Leading the Way
to
Assessment *for* Learning:
A Practical Guide

Second Edition

A Joint Publication

Solution Tree

Connections
Publishing

Leading the Way
to
Assessment *for* Learning:
A Practical Guide

Second Edition

Anne Davies, Ph.D.

Sandra Herbst

Beth Parrott Reynolds, Ph.D.

Foreword by Jay McTighe

Published in the US by Solution Tree Press
555 North Morton Street
Bloomington, IN 47404

800.733.6786 (toll free) / 812.336.7700
FAX: 812.336.7790

email: info@solution-tree.com
solution-tree.com

Printed in the United States of America
15   2   3   4   5

Library of Congress Cataloging-in-Publication Data

Davies, Anne, 1955-
  Leading the way to assessment for learning : a practical guide / Anne Davies, Sandra Herbst,
Beth Parrott Reynolds ; foreword by Jay McTighe. -- 2nd ed.
      p. cm.
  Rev. ed. of: Leading the way to making classroom assessment work., c2008.
  "Joint Publication Solution Tree Connections Publishing."
  Includes bibliographical references and index.
  ISBN 978-1-935543-94-7 (perfect bound : alk. paper) -- ISBN 978-1-935543-95-4 (library
edition : alk. paper)
  1. Educational tests and measurements. I. Herbst, Sandra, 1970- II. Reynolds, Beth Parrott,
1954- III. Davies, Anne, 1955- Leading the way to making classroom assessment work. IV. Title.
  LB3051.D365 2011b
  371.26--dc23
                          2011045467

Solution Tree
Jeffrey C. Jones, CEO & President

Solution Tree Press
President: Douglas M. Rife
Publisher: Robert D. Clouse
Vice President of Production: Gretchen Knapp
Managing Production Editor: Caroline Wise

Connections Publishing
Project Manager: Judith Hall-Patch
Editor: Annie Jack
Design: Beachwalker Studio, Ken Chong, Mackenzie Duncan, Kelly Giordano, Cori Jones

Contents

Dedicated to our hardworking and inspiring colleagues and in memory of the many fine educators who are no longer with us.

Foreword

This book begins with a brief history of naval navigational aids, from the astrolabe, to the sextant, to modern Global Positioning Systems (GPS). Indeed, this opening provides an apt metaphor since Anne Davies and her co-authors ably navigate readers through the often-foggy seas of educational assessment. Initial clarity is provided by the important distinction between assessment *of* learning and assessment *for* learning. While acknowledging the former, the authors concentrate on the latter. In fact, one might summarize the book's content through these essential questions: In what ways can classroom assessment practices enhance learning, not simply measure it? And what is the leader's role in this important work?

While each major section includes a synthesis and summary of relevant research on learning and classroom assessment, the book does not dwell on theory. Instead, the emphasis is pragmatic; i.e., research is considered in terms of its implications and applications to daily practice. *Leading the Way* offers a variety of practical and proven ideas to guide leaders in using assessment to support the teaching of students, the learning of adults, and their own work as educational leaders. To do this, leaders must be principal teachers—diagnose prior knowledge and skill, check learning along the way, and provide descriptive feedback for improving learning. In addition, the book suggests ways in which leaders can actively engage their learners in the assessment process by involving them in establishing criteria and rubrics, examining models, self-assessing their work, and taking responsibility for communicating results and setting goals. Personalized vignettes of actual students and adult learners bring these learning-enhancing assessment practices to life.

Leading the Way also includes specific suggestions to administrators interested in fostering an assessment *for* learning culture throughout their schools. The authors present sensible ideas to academic leaders for helping their staff examine assessment results and make necessary adjustments to improve their instruction and student learning. They include helpful discussions on conducting classroom observations, orchestrating professional development, and involving parents in the assessment process as well as ways for leaders to model the ideas in their work.

As a reader of this book, you will come away with a deeper understanding of the principles of assessment *for* learning and the practices to actualize these ideas. So, join Davies and her co-authors as they *lead the way*. You and your colleagues will enjoy the journey, and all learners will reap the benefits.

Jay McTighe

Preface

Until the 1800s, the astrolabe was considered an amazing navigational instrument for determining a ship's position and for charting a course to its destination. When the sextant was invented, it gave navigators a more accurate tool, by measuring celestial objects in relation to the horizon rather than itself. The recent development of the GPS (Global Positioning System) has given us a whole new capacity to measure where we are on this planet. Using feedback information relayed from three orbiting satellites, the distance is calculated by trilateration to give a phenomenally accurate gauge of time and position. This ability to see ourselves from a global perspective has become a paradigm for how we relate to our lives.

Recently, leaders are developing new tracking systems for determining the path of education, with an eye for the future. Traditional assessment and reporting systems no longer meet the needs of teachers or students in preparing them for their learning journey. Today young people must be independent and self-directed in their education, since they are more likely to have many careers throughout their lifetime. Involving them in the classroom assessment process gives them the tools to chart their own learning course.

Research has shown that involving students in classroom assessment results in considerable gains in achievement, "amongst the largest ever reported for educational interventions" (Black and Wiliam 1998, p. 61). Because of this, educators are seeking new tools to help them identify where students are on their learning journey and give them the information they need to take their next steps. Quality classroom assessment uses triangulation of evidence and feedback from teachers, parents, and students themselves to help educators and students assess the learning that is taking place (assessment *for* learning). Furthermore, it gives information for taking next steps, as well as collecting the evidence needed to account for learning (assessment *of* learning).

Leading the Way to Assessment for *Learning: A Practical Guide* is important because it describes the principles of assessment *for* learning in the classroom and in our work as leaders. Knowing what classroom assessment looks like, sounds like, and feels like in the classroom is important to the work of principals, assistant principals, curriculum coordinators, assistant superintendents, and CEOs, such as superintendents or directors. Lead learners know that although their job assignment may not bring them into the classroom on a daily basis, it is still critical to deeply understand the teaching and learning process so they can use assessment *for* learning to support the learning of adults, schools, and the system as a whole.

As you consider supporting teachers in refining and renewing their classroom assessment practices, don't be deceived by how simple it appears to be to involve students in assessment *for* learning. The ideas themselves are simple, but implementing them in today's busy classrooms will take some time. One of your roles is to assure teachers that the time spent improving classroom assessment will be well worthwhile in terms of student learning and achievement.

Leading the Way to Assessment for *Learning: A Practical Guide* is important because it describes the principles of assessment *for* learning in the classroom and in our work as leaders.

Each chapter includes:

- A detailed description of assessment at the classroom level
- Indicators of the classroom-based application of key assessment *for* learning principles
- Strategies to support classroom teachers in their learning
- Ways to consider modeling key principles in your own work as a lead learner
- Ways to continue to learn how to better "walk the talk"

On a CBC Radio broadcast, Canadian journalist and author Rita Shelton Deverell (1994) defined an expert as "a person who has a deep understanding of his or her own personal experience." As you work with the ideas in this book, consider yourself invited to develop your own expertise in the area of assessment *for* learning, so you can help those around you grow. While you are thinking through the issues, becoming familiar with the research, making your decisions, and working with your students, your teachers, and your leadership team, you will find your own ways to make assessment *for* learning work. The journey to better quality classroom assessment is too important to

miss.

Leading the Way to Assessment for *Learning: A Practical Guide* involves the following steps:

- Build a foundation for assessment (chapter 2).
- Help learners understand what they are to learn (chapter 3).
- Use samples to show what the learning could look like (chapter 4).
- Decide what counts as evidence (chapter 5).
- Involve learners in classroom assessment (chapter 6).
- Make assessment–learning connections (chapter 7).
- Involve learners in collecting, organizing, and presenting evidence (chapter 8).
- Involve learners in communicating about learning (chapter 9).
- Rethink evaluation and reporting (chapter 10).
- Deepen our own and others' understanding about assessment *for* learning (chapter 11).

This book, along with its companion, *Transforming Schools and Systems Using Assessment: A Practical Guide*, can help you to put into practice the principles and big ideas of assessment *for* learning. Whether your system is a school, a cluster of schools, a department, or an entire district or system (state, province, territory, or country), we invite you to actively take on the role of learner—to allow assessment *for* learning not only to help guide your leadership of others, but to experience the journey on your own learning path.

Assessment in the Service of Learning

"In a time of drastic change it is the learners who inherit the future. The learned usually find themselves equipped to live in a world that no longer exists."

Eric Hoffer

Transforming information into knowledge is a key task of leadership. Leaders need to know how to use all kinds of assessment information and processes in support of learning. Leaders need to understand and use information appropriately. One source of information for leaders is large-scale assessment information data, such as PISA, TIMSS, and state or provincial assessments. These are lagging indicators, which tell you the impact of the decisions made *after* it is too late to change. The lessons of the Great Depression, the latest economic downturn, stock market crash, or big business failure arrived too late for the people impacted by them. Moreover, the actual events and decisions that led to these disasters will never be repeated again in exactly the same way or in the same context. Therefore, although history has much to teach us, the lessons of the past will never be a road map to the future.

Large-scale assessment provides leaders with a history lesson. By the time those large-scale assessment scores arrive, the opportunity to change the learning for individual students has passed. Time spent analyzing the data may yield some general ideas about how to improve the learning for groups of students; however, the information won't make a difference for those students who have now moved on. Nor is it likely to make a difference for future students, unless the data are carefully analyzed. Consider the following example.

Chapter 1

Contents

Here is a set of large-scale assessment scores from an anonymous large jurisdiction reported between 2005 and 2009 for more than 125,000 students at one grade level:

Chart of Published Scores				
	Year A	Year B	Year C	Year D
Reading	62%	62%	61%	61%
Writing	64%	64%	66%	68%
Mathematics	68%	64%	68%	68%

First, notice how little change has taken place over four years at a cost of between $32–50 million per year. This system can claim a 0–4% increase in reading (1% change), writing (4% change), and mathematics (0% change). In fact, looking only at these numbers, one might think the teachers and schools in this jurisdiction aren't working hard enough to improve. Leaders know the difference between politics and pedagogy. We refrain from making a judgment since the table in this report doesn't give enough information. The technical reports explain the accuracy and "error of measurement" for this same information/data. They show that individual student scores range in accuracy from .79 to .82. Notice that these "error of measurement" rates are less accurate than the latest political poll your news station reports. What kind of decisions can a leader make based on this information?

Research Connection:

Ask yourself whether the $32–50 million spent annually over the past 14 years this jurisdiction has been engaged in large-scale assessment could have been used in better ways. Research shows that investing in classroom assessment has a greater impact on student learning (Crooks 1988; Black and Wiliam 1998), and further, that informed teachers' professional judgment is more reliable and valid than external assessment (ARG 2005).

Now there are two problems emerging. First, individual student scores may show mastery (or not) in error. For example, if a score of 50 represented mastery, then a typical error of measurement rate tells us that the actual score could have been anything from 46 to 54. This means that decisions can only be based on actual student scores. Second, if the reported data are lumped together—that is, "Writing" rather than specifics such as "Ideas, Meaning, Organization, Voice, Word Choice, or Conventions"—then you won't have enough information to know where you need to target your action. The feedback is too general to be of use in making a difference.

What does this mean to leaders? It means that when you are analyzing large-scale assessment data for your school or for different classrooms, you have to be very careful. Given the typical reported error of measurement, any score within the range reported could be the right one. Yes, it's true. Your arbitrarily selected score for any student from the possible range, given error of measurement, is just as likely to be correct as the reported score. That is the impact of error of measurement. Further, the failure to accurately report and consider the impact of the error of measurement is inadvertently compounded by leaders. Leaders don't have good information until they analyze it. The procedures used to gather the information data are *not* free of error, and therefore the scores are not accurate unless reported as a range of possibility.

Researchers have continued to document that this type of large-scale assessment data is *wrong* "one out of five times" (ARG 2006). The information you need is in the fine print of the technical reports that accompany large-scale assessments. This means that a student score of 68 might actually have been 64 or as high as 72. No one knows. All large-scale assessment data have similar problems. To be the kind of leader you need to be in these times, you must read the technical reports that explain how your jurisdiction's information data are being collected. Look for reported accuracy rates. What is the error of measurement? Do the simple arithmetic to calculate the range of the scores of your students and report the information as close to the actual content of the standard or outcome as possible—avoid general feedback. Research from many sources shows general feedback does *not* lead to learning (Davies 2004; Hattie 2008; Hattie and Timperley 2007; Shute 2008).

Educators can make use of the information that comes from large-scale assessment when it comes to trends and patterns across a system, as long as leaders use individual student data very carefully. Leaders do need to know that large-scale assessment data *do not* give the kind of information that informs the day-by-day or month-by-month work of classrooms, schools, and groups of schools.

On the other hand, assessment *for* learning, when done well, is truly assessment *in the service of* student learning. Classroom assessment data inform the minute-by-minute, day-by-day, and month-by-month work of schools. They have the greatest impact on student learning of any educational innovation ever documented (Black and Wiliam 1998). The data show that all students improve, with struggling learners— the ones who have the greatest learning needs—showing the greatest gains.

To put this into perspective, large-scale assessment, as documented by the jurisdictions, could be reported as giving leaders the wrong data one out of five times at a cost of billions. That means, if you have a class of 25 students, you could get wrong information about the learning of *five* of them, if you rely only on large-scale assessment results. Further, only classroom teachers know which five students, and only if they've collected evidence of learning from multiple sources over time. When leaders spend time supporting teachers to improve their professional judgment, the quality of information data improves (ARG 2006).

In order to use all information well, a leader needs to know the strengths and weaknesses of each kind of data. In general, classroom assessment provides frequent information that can inform the work of all adults in support of student learning; large-scale assessments can provide periodic information that tells you the trend and pattern across large numbers of students.

Used well, classroom and large-scale assessment can work together to provide balance and serve leaders by providing the kind of information leaders can turn into knowledge.

School and system leaders need to support teachers to use the process of assessment *for* learning day-by-day to support their students' learning. Also, it is important that leaders work with teachers to use classroom information—collected formally and informally—to inform decision making for both individuals and groups at frequent intervals.

When it comes to classroom assessment, the terms *assessment* and *evaluation* are often used interchangeably, but they have different meanings. When teachers engage in *assessment*, they are gathering information about student learning that informs their teaching and helps students learn more. This may involve an assessment task or examining student work (looking at products, observing process, and listening to and talking with students). Teachers may teach differently, based on what they discover as they assess.

Evaluation is a process of reviewing the evidence and determining its value. When teachers evaluate, they decide whether or not students have learned what they needed to learn and how well they have learned it. They make a professional judgment. This process is also referred to as "summative evaluation"—summing up the achievement. This professional judgment is often communicated to others in the form of grades on student work, or on report cards at the end of the term.

The importance of using classroom assessment data and using it well needs to be emphasized. To illustrate the difference between classroom assessment and classroom evaluation, the following scenario was originally developed by Michael Burger:

Three students are taking a course in how to pack a parachute. Imagine that the class average is represented by a horizontal line. Student Number One initially scored very high, but his scores have dropped as the end of the course approaches. Student Number Two's evaluations are erratic. Sometimes he does very well, and sometimes he doesn't. The teacher has a hard time predicting from day to day how he will do. Student Number

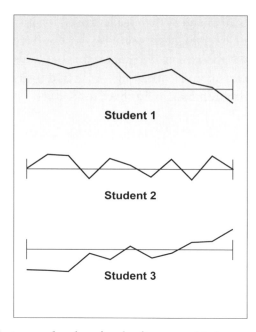

Student 1

Student 2

Student 3

Three did very poorly in relation to the class for the first two-thirds of the course, but has lately figured out how to successfully pack a parachute.

Which of these students would you want to pack your parachute? Number One? Number Two? Number Three? Most people would choose Number Three. The problem is that Number Three did not pass the course. When his grades were tallied and averaged, they weren't high enough. Number One and Number Two did pass.

If the class took place in a norm-referenced assessment system, then what matters is not what is learned, but how students do compared to each other. They could all have failed to learn, but there would still be a first, second, and third in the class! If this class were taking place now in K–12 public education in North America, it would be criterion-referenced or standards-based. That means it is important that all students learn—that is, come to understand what they need to know, do, and be able to articulate, given the learning standards or outcomes. Students are evaluated in relation to how well they know, can do, and articulate their knowledge, understanding, and application of the standards or outcomes they are to learn.

Think about it. In a standards-based system where all students are expected to learn at high levels, the decision to assess or to evaluate is an important one. The research is clear—if evaluation occurs too frequently, students will not be as successful as they could be (Crooks 1988; Black and Wiliam 1998). This is particularly true of students who struggle. When should teachers assess, and when should teachers evaluate? What might be the results of evaluating too early or too much? How do teachers know if they are evaluating the right things? How do they know what makes sense for the learner and for the course? These are important questions for us to consider and the best response is situation dependent—that is, it depends on the context, including what is best for the learners, what makes sense given the learning expectations, and how much time remains until reporting time.

It is obvious that when students are acquiring and constructing new skills, knowledge, and understanding, they need a chance to practice. This is part of the learning process. Assessment *for* learning, a term used to describe this process, involves:

- Checking to see what has been learned and what needs to be learned next
- Accessing specific and descriptive feedback in relation to criteria that is focused on improvement
- Involving students in their own assessment

Assessment *in the service of* learning provides information that will be used by teachers to inform their next teaching steps and used by students to guide their next learning steps. It is not enough for assessment information to be only available to teachers, when students also need that information in order to learn.

A Classroom Assessment Process That Works

There are three general parts to a classroom assessment process that works. First, teachers review the curriculum and standards documents and describe for themselves the learning that students are expected to accomplish. They collect and review samples and models that show what the learning looks like for students of a particular age range, and they think through the kinds of evidence their students could produce to show they have mastered what they needed to learn.

Second, once the big picture is established, teachers work with students to bring them into the assessment process. They do this by talking about the learning, showing samples and discussing what the evidence might look like, setting criteria with students, engaging in activities such as self-assessment, peer assessment, and goal setting, and collecting evidence or proof of their learning to deepen their understanding. They present their work to others and receive more feedback. This cycle continues as students are involved in revising criteria and continuing their learning. As students participate in assessment, they become partners in the continuous assessment *for* learning cycle.

Third, teachers evaluate; they "sum up" the learning (summative evaluation). At this time they look at all the evidence of learning collected by students and by the teacher from multiple sources over time and make a judgment regarding the degree to which students have learned what they need to learn.

Research Connection:

When students are involved in their own assessment, mistakes become feedback they can use to adjust what they are doing. When students' mistakes are identified by others, and feedback is limited to grades or scores, students are less likely to know what to do differently next time (Black and Wiliam 1998; Butler and Nisan 1986; Butler 1987; Shepard and Smith 1986, 1987).

Being a Leader

Indicators of Classroom Application

Classroom assessment *for* learning is successful when all students—
even those who typically struggle—are learning, and when classroom
teachers are using assessment to ensure all students are learning and
achieving at high levels.

Here are some questions to guide leaders' observations in the
classroom:

- How do teachers articulate the difference between criterion-
referenced assessment and norm-referenced assessment and
illustrate how that difference is taken into account in their
assessment and evaluation process?
- How do you assess whether or not teachers understand the
difference between assessment and evaluation?
- How are teachers planning to involve the student—the person
most able to improve the learning—deeply in the assessment
process?

Supporting Classroom Teachers

Lead learners need to *support* teachers as they work to improve
classroom assessment. Leaders are asking questions such as, "What
does quality classroom assessment look like? What do I look for? How
can I support classroom teachers in their learning journey? How can I
model and be the lead learner I aspire to be?"

Leaders can support classroom teachers by asking them to reflect
on what they already know and what they would like to learn more
about, and by finding ways to share these key ideas. For example, lead

learners are using *Making Classroom Assessment Work* (3rd edition) as a focus for learning and studying about assessment *for* learning and engaging adult learners in conversation. Leaders ask questions such as:

1. When you consider quality classroom assessment as it is described here, what do you think? Do you feel that some of your practices have been confirmed? Are there new ideas? Any reminders? Give examples as you describe your work in this area.

2. Is there something you would like to learn more about? Talk with someone else about your thinking. Record your ideas. What would a relevant learning plan for this year look like for you? How can I help?

3. Invite teachers to spend time engaged in the "Guiding Our Own Learning" and "Guiding the Learning of Students" tasks at the end of each chapter in *Making Classroom Assessment Work*. When completed, the end-of-chapter tasks result in a draft assessment plan for one subject area. Chapter 1 tasks are on the facing page.

4. Consider how to spend the valuable time available for professional learning. It might be helpful to spend a little time reviewing large-scale assessment scores. Yes, it might also be valuable to review the occasional common assessment data. Research says the most benefit will come from reviewing collections of student work collected over time from multiple sources in relation to the learning destination (see chapter 5 for more on this topic).

If you want to make a difference, right now, for today's learners, then classroom assessment is your leadership priority. The decision is yours.

Guiding Our Own Learning

You already know some things about classroom assessment. I invite you to think about what you would like to add to your assessment practices and what you might like to stop doing, so you have time to do the new thing well.

1. Begin by thinking about what you have read so far. Has it confirmed some things for you? Did you realize you were already doing some of this? Did it remind you of anything you had forgotten?

2. Record something you would like to learn more about. Talk with someone else about your thinking.

Guiding the Learning of Students

As you prepare students to assess their way to success, consider asking them about assessment. Pose questions, such as:

- What is the best way to show what you know?
- How do you learn best?
- What helps you remember?
- What kind of feedback helps your learning?
- Do you like to learn and practice by yourself or with others?

Listening to learners informs our teaching practice.

From © 2011 *Making Classroom Assessment Work* (3rd edition) by Anne Davies, p. 14.

In preparing teachers to work with students, leaders can encourage them to reflect on their own learning, just as they are asking their students to do. Consider posing similar questions, such as:

- What are all the possible ways for students to show what they know?
- How do you learn best? How do your students learn?
- What helps you remember? What helps students remember?
- What kind of feedback helps your learning? What kind of feedback works for your students?

Research Matters

Why involve students? Why consider revisiting classroom assessment and the role of summative assessment? Recent research in this area is clearly pointing towards needed changes. What is the key classroom assessment research that every school leader needs to know about? There are seven important research studies focused on assessment that have often been missed by those planning to measure student achievement and set policies to encourage best teaching and assessment practices.

1. Butler (1987, 1988) conducted experimental design studies and found that student work receiving grades and marks (with or without feedback) was clearly associated with decreasing student achievement, while specific feedback without grades and marks was clearly associated with increasing achievement.

2. Black and Wiliam (1998) summarized classroom assessment research conducted internationally over a ten-year period. Their findings explain the power of classroom assessment and its role in improving learning. They detailed the significant learning achievements students experience—especially struggling students— when assessment *for* learning techniques are employed. Key strategies include setting clear success criteria, increasing specific, descriptive feedback, and decreasing summarized, evaluative feedback such as grades and marks.

3. Harlen and Deakin Crick (2003), studying the role of tests and motivation to learn, found that students who do less well on tests and evaluations of any kind tend to be less motivated and, as a result, do even less well on subsequent tests and evaluations. Based on their research, they strongly recommend that students be engaged in assessment *for* learning activities—such as setting criteria, giving and receiving feedback, and collecting evidence of learning—in order to increase achievement levels, as well as motivation to learn.

4. Meisels et al.'s (2003) study examined the impact of curriculum-embedded performance assessment on students' subsequent performance on the Iowa Tests of Basic Skills (ITBS). The researchers note that obtaining continuous information about students during the learning and engaging students as active participants in the classroom assessment process enhances teaching and improves learning.

5. Rodriguez (2004) "evaluated the relationship between assessment practices and achievement and the mediated roles of students' self-efficacy and effort" (p. 1). Rodriguez found that teachers' classroom assessment practices have a significant relationship to classroom performance. Classroom assessment practices include writing assignments, data collection activities, long- and short-term individual projects, oral reports, worksheets, homework, journal writing, quizzes, tests, observations, student responses in class, and externally created exams that were used to give feedback, group students, diagnose learning problems, and plan future lessons.

6. The Assessment Reform Group in the UK commissioned a series of studies examining summative assessment. Working Papers 1, 2, and 3 are available (ARG-ASF Project, 2005: http://k1.ioe.ac.uk/tlrp/arg/ASF.html). They found when teachers work with each other and review evidence of student learning to determine whether or not students are meeting the standards with sufficient quality, teachers become more confident and better able to make independent judgments. Further, the reliability of teachers' assessment increases when teachers participate in developing criteria, have some ownership of them, and understand the language used. Teachers who learn to assess student work as part of external summative assessment processes using clearly specified criteria improve the quality of their classroom assessment.

7. "Formative Assessment—Improving Student Learning in Secondary Classrooms" (Center for Educational Research and Innovation 2005), a report based on research findings and classroom-level observations in 8 countries (Australia [Queensland], Denmark, England, Finland, Italy, New Zealand, Scotland, and some provinces in Canada) concluded that classroom assessment that supports student learning:

   • Establishes a classroom culture that encourages interaction and the use of assessment tools
   • Establishes learning goals, and tracks individual student progress toward those goals
   • Uses varied instruction methods to meet diverse student needs
   • Uses varied approaches to assessing student understanding
   • Provides feedback on student performance and adaptation of instruction to meet identified needs
   • Involves students actively in the learning and assessment process

The research is compelling. School leaders intending to make a difference for students need to focus on classroom assessment.

Adapted from A. Davies, "Leading Towards Learning and Achievement" in J. Burger, C. Webber, and P. Klinck (Eds.) 2007. *Intelligent Leadership: Constructs for Thinking Education Leaders*. Secaucus, NJ: Springer Publishers.

A print-friendly copy of Research Matters can be found on page 164 of appendix 2.

Being a Lead Learner

Lead learners, whether at the school or district level, must understand and be able to recognize what they are asking others to know, do, and articulate. This includes classroom assessment practices that engage students in their own learning. Lead learners at the school level also need to know how to support teachers in increasing their craft knowledge regarding assessment. Lead learners at the district level, including superintendents and assistant superintendents, must know what both the teachers and administrators require as they continue to learn in this area. Though they may be physically removed from the daily life of the classroom, opportunities for closer and deeper understanding are important.

Lead learners are prepared to learn alongside others, making public their emerging learning challenges. Though they may not have a classroom of students, they provide a model in their own practice of the "big ideas" and principles of assessment *for* learning. When leaders mindfully use assessment with the adult learners they serve, everyone achieves more. Walking the talk requires changing habits.

When it comes to assessment, change isn't only for classroom teachers. It is also important that we, as lead learners, keep up with the research. Throughout this book and its companion volume, *Transforming Schools and Systems Using Assessment: A Practical Guide*, is a collection of research notes. We encourage you to read the research summaries and to further explore the original works (see pages 149–162).

Research Connection:

When students are involved in their own assessment, their self-assessments help teachers design instruction to better meet the needs of learners (Anthony, Johnson, Mickelson, and Preece 1991; Andrade 2011; Boud 1995; Davies, Cameron, Politano, and Gregory 1992; Elbow 1986; Preece 1995; Wiggins 1993).

Planning to Walk the Talk

As you consider the ideas in this chapter with your leadership colleagues and by yourself, keep a list of what being a lead learner looks like, so it can serve as a record of your learning journey in terms of quality assessment. Take a few minutes to think about your vision and what you already do daily in your job that models quality assessment with your adult learners. Record your thoughts. Date your work. This list can serve as a simple, yet powerful, baseline sample of your growth in the area of classroom assessment. Place your work in your draft portfolio collection.

Building the Foundation for Quality Assessment

"Communities of the mind are collections of individuals who are bonded together by natural will and to a set of ideas and ideals."

Thomas Sergiovanni

As leaders, we need to highlight the importance of teachers carefully building a classroom environment that supports learning and quality assessment. In order for all students, no matter what their learning challenges, to fully participate in their learning and assessment, students need a safe school environment in which to learn. This includes a classroom community of learners where students know what matters and learn ways to get along with others. When teachers create classroom communities that are safe for learners, students are more likely to take risks necessary for learning. This type of community develops when learners know how to *give* help, how to *get* help, *what* help to get, and *how* to use the help to improve their learning. Classroom assessment strategies provide the means to accomplish all this as teachers and students co-construct criteria for classroom routines, quality work, and getting along with one another. As teachers take their first steps with students, it is essential that they take time to:

- Emphasize that mistakes are essential for learning
- Help students understand the differences between descriptive and evaluative feedback
- Understand that learning takes time
- Appreciate that success has many different looks
- Communicate these ideas to parents and others
- Create a caring community of learners

Mistakes Are Essential for Learning

Learning involves taking risks and making mistakes, and then doing things differently as a result. Mistakes provide assessment evidence—they give learners feedback about what is not working and bring them closer to knowing what will work. Unless teachers help students understand that mistakes are essential for learning, students may not be willing to take the risks necessary for learning.

The Difference Between Descriptive and Evaluative Feedback

Learners understand feedback. It is what they get when they try to shoot a basket and make it or don't make it. It is what happens when someone laughs as they share a funny story. It is what the teacher gives when students finish an assignment or turn in their homework. What students don't usually understand is that there are different types of feedback—descriptive feedback and evaluative feedback.

Descriptive feedback is best during the learning time as it gives learners information about their learning that helps them self-reference and plan their next steps. This type of feedback:

- Comes *during* as well as *after* the learning
- Is easily understood and relates directly to the learning
- Is specific, so performance can improve
- Involves choice on the part of the learner as to the type of feedback and how to receive it
- Is part of an ongoing conversation about the learning
- Is in comparison to models, exemplars, samples, or descriptions
- Is about the performance or the work—not the person

Evaluative feedback is more appropriate at the end of learning. It tells the learner how she or he has performed as compared to others (norm-referenced assessment) or as compared to what was to be learned (criterion-referenced assessment). Evaluative feedback is often reported using grades, numbers, checks, or other symbols. Because evaluative feedback has been encoded into a summary comment ("great job"), a grade, or symbol of some kind (B, 72%, 3), students usually understand whether they need to improve but not *how* to improve. Unless specific, descriptive feedback is also provided, students may not have enough information to understand what they need to do in order to improve. When evaluative feedback is present, struggling students may not attend to the descriptive feedback (Butler 1988). Successful students seem better able to decode the evaluative feedback and use the information to support their learning (Brookhart 2001).

Research Connection:

Seminal feedback research is finding that the feedback that best supports student learning is specific and descriptive. It tells students what to do more of and what to do less of. It does not include coded evaluative feedback such as grades, marks, or other encoded information (Black and Wiliam 1998; Butler 1987, 1988).

Time to Learn

In order to learn, students need time to process. This is because meaning (learning) is only generated from within (Jensen 1998). When we have more time to think about our learning, we learn more. When teachers are pressured to cover the curriculum on a tight schedule, they often don't take time to let students do the processing they need in order to learn. When students are encouraged to talk about their learning and to self-assess in relation to criteria, models, or exemplars, they learn to give themselves descriptive feedback that helps them learn more.

When teachers slow down and involve students, students are more likely to understand what they are to learn and what it looks like, and more learning takes place. When students have time to think about their learning and decide what needs to be changed or improved, they can set goals.

Students need time to:

- Set and use criteria
- Self-assess
- Receive and give descriptive feedback

- Collect proof or evidence of learning
- Set and reset their goals
- Seek specific support for their learning
- Communicate their learning to others

It takes time to involve students in the assessment process. Teachers need to start slowly. Doing things more than once is also essential for learning. It is when students do something the second and third time that they come to understand what they know and what they need to know. Students need practice time to learn. Through repetition, they are able to take what they are learning and apply it at deeper and deeper levels.

Research Connection:

Co-constructing criteria changes the teaching and learning environment. Having criteria results in more students being engaged and learning at higher levels (Joslin 2002; Schmoker 1996; Thome 2001; Young 2000).

Success Has Many Different Looks

Students learn in different ways and at different rates; there will never be a class where all the students are the same. Thus, if teachers provide only a few options for students to demonstrate their learning, they can limit students' ability or opportunity to show what they know. Excellence can be revealed in a multitude of ways. As diversity increases among our students, whether from learning styles, culture and language, family circumstances, or countless other factors, teachers need to learn how to allow for differences and to work toward students meeting standards. Then, diversity can be a source of strength in our communities and in our classrooms.

Evidence of learning needs to be diverse because it requires performance and self-assessment or reflection to demonstrate application and the ability to articulate understandings. This means that written work or test results can never be enough. Observing application of knowledge, listening to students articulate understandings, and engaging students in demonstrating acquisition of knowledge are valid evidence. Teachers need a range of evidence. Our challenge is to imagine the possibilities for proof of learning that can include all students.

Involving Parents

Part of the foundation for classroom assessment is effective communication with parents and others who support students' learning. Teachers build relationships that extend beyond the classroom through invitations to share information, goal-setting conferences, and checking in. As they work with students, teachers involve and inform parents in various ways, such as:

- Sending emails to parents about the day's learning and questions to ask their child
- Having students maintain a website featuring the learning in class
- Selecting key work samples to show parents in person, online, or at school
- Working with parents to set goals and to collect evidence of working toward achieving the goals

Research Connection:

> When parents are involved in talking about learning with their children, children achieve more. The more parents are involved, the higher the student achievement levels (Henderson and Berla 1994).

A Community of Learners

Relationships are key. When teachers begin by sharing the learning destination with students and parents and by building classroom agreements, they help build a community where learning is supported by assessment. Learning is only possible when everyone agrees that making mistakes, giving and receiving feedback, and taking time to self-assess and to learn are essential. Only when everyone works together can the foundation for classroom assessment—and learning—be established.

Being a Leader

Indicators of Classroom Application

There are many ways that teachers and students build powerful learning environments together. Some indicators include:

- Students are engaged in learning.
- Classroom "rules" or expectations are transformed into classroom agreements, which are developed together and posted in student language.
- Students know how to problem solve and resolve conflicts.
- Risk-taking that results in learning is apparent.
- Mistakes are valued and inform everyone's learning.
- Feedback is specific and descriptive.
- Student-created criteria are posted.
- Students have some choice around how to represent and show their learning.
- Students are involved in collecting evidence of their own learning and showing it to parents and teachers.

Supporting Classroom Teachers

Consider providing time as a faculty to read chapter 2 in *Making Classroom Assessment Work,* and then complete the "Guiding Our Own Learning" and "Guiding the Learning of Students" tasks at the end of the chapter. Chapter 2 tasks are on the facing page.

Guiding Our Own Learning

Think of a time when you learned something successfully. Make some notes about what you learned, when and where you learned it, who helped you, how they helped, and what kind of feedback you got. Talk with others about your experiences.

Build a common list of the kinds of feedback you found supportive for your learning. Talk about the implications for your students' learning and your teaching.

Take time to reflect. How can you use this information to help your students learn more? How can you begin to give up responsibility for being the main source of feedback in the classroom? How can you create opportunities for students to get feedback for themselves that helps their learning?

Guiding the Learning of Students

As a group, ask students to brainstorm their responses to the following question: What counts in quality work?

Then, as individuals, ask students to respond to the following question in writing: What kind of feedback helps me do a better job? Give examples and explain why.

Reflect on their responses, considering whether your students are well-served by their notions of quality and their understanding of feedback for learning.

You might want to spend some time sharing the research around feedback with them and talking about your expectations of what they need to know, be able to do, and articulate in order to produce quality work.

From © 2011 *Making Classroom Assessment Work* (3rd edition) by Anne Davies, p. 24

Consider taking time to have a thoughtful dialogue with your classroom and leadership colleagues about learning, teaching, and classroom assessment. Two starting points are *beliefs clarification* and *learning more about feedback*.

Beliefs Clarification

The following process is designed to help participants uncover the beliefs that guide their day-to-day work. When these are identified, individuals can decide whether a belief is one that supports their work or whether they want to reconsider a belief they currently hold because it does not, in their opinion, support their work. This process is designed to uncover beliefs, not to force people to change them, although it often leads to clarification and adjustments in behavior. As our beliefs emerge from our experiences—both examined and unexamined—it is important to stress that it is inappropriate to judge another's beliefs as either good or bad. A sample belief statement is pictured here.

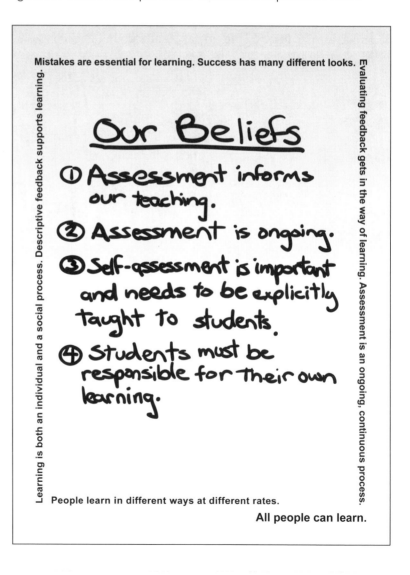

Part One:
Working in small groups, set ground rules or norms for collaboration together.

Part Two:
Ask participants to take three to five minutes to work by themselves quietly and list their beliefs about teaching, learning, assessment, and evaluation. After five minutes, ask members of each small group to take turns sharing their beliefs, making note of any the group holds in common. Record those commonly held beliefs on chart paper to share with the larger group. Post for information.

Part Three:
Divide the participants into groups of three. Ask each group to engage in a process of beliefs clarification. There are no right or wrong answers. The process is simple:

> First person states a belief.
>
> Second person restates what has been said and says, "Please tell me why. . .?"
>
> First person explains further.
>
> Second person restates and says, "Please tell me why . . . ?" (Repeat at least twice.)
>
> Observer listens and when it is done, shares what she/he noticed.
>
> Then participants change roles and repeat the process.

Provide enough time for each person to share one or more beliefs. Consider revisiting this process periodically. Encourage participants to continue clarifying their own beliefs with a trusted colleague or through journal writing. Requesting that staff members include their beliefs as part of a professional learning portfolio can be a helpful way to provide yet another purpose for this work.

This activity provides time for participants to consider what they already know about feedback, and to think about how they can apply what they already know to working with learners.

Say to the group, "Think of a time when you learned something successfully. Make some notes about what you learned, when and where you learned it, who helped you, how they helped, and what kind of feedback you got."

After participants have had time to make some notes, it is time to debrief as a small group. Suggest that participants talk with others about their experiences and build a common list of the kinds of feedback they found that supported their learning. Ask them to talk about the implications for learning and teaching.

Following the small group's discussion, encourage participants to share their ideas with the large group. Record the list on chart paper. Finally, ask them to reflect on one or more of the following questions:

- How can you use this information to help *your* students learn more?
- How can you provide more feedback for learning?
- How can you begin to give up responsibility for being the main source of feedback?
- How can you create opportunities for learners to get feedback for themselves that helps their learning?

Understanding quality feedback is different than actually giving quality feedback. Invite participants to set goals to improve the quality of feedback for their own students. Encourage them to find ways for students to give themselves feedback, so teachers are working smarter, not harder. Invite them to partner with a colleague to do a feedback check periodically.

Being a Lead Learner

There are many ways leaders work together with others to build inspiring and productive work environments. If you are using assessment *for* learning principles, the following indicators will be apparent:

- Staff are engaged, enthusiastic, and busy learning.
- "Norms" for working together and getting along are developed together, are posted, and act as a touchstone prior to any meeting.
- Adults know how to go about problem solving and resolving conflicts.
- Everyone is comfortable taking some risks to learn.
- Mistakes are valued and inform everyone's learning.
- Feedback is available from multiple sources.
- Criteria are created together and posted.
- Evidence of ongoing learning and success is represented in a variety of ways.

Consider providing feedback that is specific and descriptive. After completing a walk-through of a classroom, a principal provides brief written or oral feedback that indicates what she observed the students doing in relation to co-constructing criteria focused on involving students in assessment. After visiting a school, a superintendent includes, in a follow-up conversation or note, his observations about the physical learning environment, evidence of the principal's leadership, or descriptions of exemplary classroom practice.

Leaders can encourage teachers to take time to learn more by providing opportunities to meet during the school week. Further, when designing class schedules, it is important to thoughtfully build in time for groups of teachers to meet and to learn together.

Planning to Walk the Talk

List your beliefs about teaching, learning, assessment, and evaluation.
Meet with two of your leadership colleagues and use the process
described on page 23 to clarify your own beliefs. You and your
colleagues may experience discomfort during the discussion. This
process will help you empathize with other adult learners and
understand their resistance to uncovering and discussing personal
beliefs. Keep your list of beliefs so you can
examine it in the future to see what change
has occurred. Place your work in your draft
portfolio collection.

Beginning With the End in Mind

"Students can reach any target that they know about and that holds still for them."

Rick Stiggins

When golfers swing their golf clubs, they know where to aim—toward the flag marking the next hole. Pilots file flight plans before getting permission to leave the ground. Successful gardeners plan for a new season knowing what they want their garden to look like. Life coaches ask us to follow a similar process when they suggest we *begin with the end in mind*. It seems obvious that reaching a destination is easier if you know where or what it is. That's the point Tyler (1949) was making over 60 years ago, when he said that the first question a teacher needs to answer is: What do I want my students to learn? Answering that question has been harder than we thought.

In North American education, the terms *standards* or *learning outcomes* refer to that which students are expected to learn (and by which they will be judged). Standards and learning outcomes provide both opportunity as well as challenge. They are a guide for teaching and for student learning. When teachers and students know where they are going, they are more likely to achieve success. When teachers know what needs to be learned and what students already know, they can plan a variety of learning pathways for students. Furthermore, students can provide a variety of evidence of having met the standard or achieved the learning outcome. Standards pose a challenge when quality expectations are unclear, when students arrive in class with differing levels of expertise, and when test results are all that matter. Challenges can become opportunities, with careful planning and thought.

Researchers reporting brain-based research (Langer 1997; Pert 1999; Pinker 1997; Restak 2003) say that when we know what we're going to be doing, we mentally prepare ourselves and activate more of our brain by doing so. Once students know what they are supposed to be

Contents

Profile of a 7th grade Math Student
· has mastered basic operations
· produces quality work
· can communicate mathematical ideas effectively
· is able to solve problems
· can represent mathematical situations in multiple ways
· gives logical arguments defending their answers
· makes connections within and outside of mathematics
· knows when to use appropriate tools in math
· is able to design experiments & surveys to collect, organize, and analyze data

learning, they can self-monitor, make adjustments, and learn more. From the teacher's point of view, there are three steps to this process:

1. Describe what students need to learn using language that students and parents will understand.
2. Share the description with students and explain how it relates to success in life outside of school.
3. Use the description to guide instruction, assessment, and evaluation.

Developing the Descriptions of the Learning Destination

For most people, writing descriptions of learning goals is harder than it looks. Teachers can start small by following three steps:

1. Choose one subject area or one unit of study for a focus.
2. Summarize the outcomes or goals in simple, clear language that corresponds to how the learning needs to be reported later.
3. Read and review the curriculum expectations for the subject and grade level, checking back to the documents to see if there is anything that was missed.

French 7

Learning Outcomes	Possible Evidence
① willingly participates in all activities (esp oral)	① checklist (observation)
② willingly takes risks	② volunteers consistently (instead of being asked)
③ positive attitude towards a 2nd language culture	③ by observation
④ shows practice of vocabulary and structures	④ tests, quizzes, daily work
⑤ works cooperatively with partner +/or small groups	⑤ observation – product production – group evaluation
⑥ shows independence in learning (uses resources)	⑥ looks in Fr/Eng dictionary before asking
⑦ can demonstrate learning visually, orally, and in writing	⑦ projects, assignments, presentations
⑧ makes connections outside of classroom + subject area	⑧ observations & projects

The accompanying examples show one group's first draft descriptions of learning outcomes for grade 7 math and French. The left column is a teacher-generated summary of curriculum learning outcomes. At this stage, it is useful to think ahead and consider possible sources of evidence.

Teachers develop descriptions of learning destinations taking into account what needs to be learned and how learning needs to be reported. Developing and using descriptions of the learning destination is part of the assessment–learning cycle. Teachers have many diverse ways of designing their descriptions to make them easy to use during the year and to align them with school and district reporting requirements. Descriptions of learning destinations vary from place to place because the context differs and each jurisdiction has its own unique vocabulary. It is helpful when teachers can work together across departments or grade levels to draft these descriptions of learning destinations so they can better communicate to students and parents in the school community. When draft versions of the learning destinations are shared across faculty, others can improve and build upon the work, saving everyone time while building confidence in the final descriptions.

Using the Learning Destination With Students

When the learning destination is made clear and the description of what needs to be learned is accompanied by samples and models that show what success looks like, students gain a better understanding of what they need to know and do. They are also better informed. This helps them to make choices that help their learning. When students know what the evidence can look like, they become more able to show teachers what they know. As teachers use detailed descriptions of the learning destination, expressed in student-friendly language (see figure below), learners find ways to better show what they know, can do, and can articulate.

Mathematics – Evidence of learning demonstrates the student . . .		
Consistently and independently:	**Usually needs some support to:**	**Needs lots of support in order to:**
• Understands, remembers, and applies mathematical concepts being studied	• Understand, remember, and apply mathematical concepts being studied	• Understand, remember, and apply mathematical concepts being studied
• Articulates clear understanding of mathematical concepts and is able to give everyday examples of use	• Articulate clear understanding of mathematical concepts and give everyday examples of use	• Articulate clear understanding of mathematical concepts and give everyday examples of use
• Applies concepts, skills, and strategies to propose solutions to problems	• Apply concepts, skills, and strategies to propose solutions to problems	• Apply concepts, skills, and strategies to propose solutions to problems
• Analyzes problems, uses a variety of effective strategies to find possible solutions, and is able to check and evaluate the effectiveness of the processes used	• Analyze problems, use a variety of effective strategies to find possible solutions, and be able to check and evaluate the effectiveness of the processes used	• Analyze problems, use a variety of effective strategies to find possible solutions, and be able to check and evaluate the effectiveness of the processes used
• Works effectively by self and with others	• Work effectively by self and with others	• Work effectively by self and with others
• Communicates effectively using words, symbols, and representations	• Communicate effectively using words, symbols, and representations	• Communicate effectively using words, symbols, and representations
• Connects ideas to self, to others, and to other ideas or tasks	• Connect ideas to self, to others, and to other ideas or tasks	• Connect ideas to self, to others, and to other ideas or tasks
• Uses mathematical habits of mind including, for example, persistence, questioning, drawing on past knowledge, precision of language, and thought	• Use mathematical habits of mind including, for example, persistence, questioning, drawing on past knowledge, precision of language, and thought	• Use mathematical habits of mind including, for example, persistence, questioning, drawing on past knowledge, precision of language, and thought
Common assessment scores: 4	Common assessment scores: 3s and 4s	Common assessment scores: mostly 3s
Evaluations such as performance tasks, projects, tests, and quizzes receive grades in the 91%–100% range.	Evaluations such as performance tasks, projects, tests, and quizzes receive grades in the 81%–90% range.	Evaluations such as performance tasks, projects, tests, and quizzes receive grades in the 71%–80% range.
Evidence of learning is demonstrated in a range of ways including: Products (e.g., work samples, tests, quizzes) Observations (e.g., class work, demonstrations, performance tasks, teacher observations) Conversations (e.g., discussions, written reflections, journal entries, conferences, interviews)		

Being a Leader

Indicators of Classroom Application

When teachers seek to ensure that all students learn, it isn't good enough to judge success by comparing to a standard that is based on high achievers' work. Success is now defined by how well *all* students are doing, not just those who typically do well. As a lead learner, look for the following indicators:

- Descriptions of success—learning destinations for each course of study—are posted in the classroom or handed out to students and parents. These descriptions reflect the standards or learning outcomes and express them in simple terms that everyone can understand.

- Students are able to answer the question, What do you need to know to be successful? by articulating the important ideas (or referring to a handout which does so) and describing how this knowledge or set of skills will be useful outside of school.

- Teachers are able to summarize the learning destination and explicitly describe how the activity, assignment, or range of activities and assignments helps *all* students learn. Furthermore, teachers can show plans for how student evidence or proof of learning will account for all the standards or outcomes.

- In response to the question, What does quality look like? students will refer to models, exemplars, or criteria.

Supporting Classroom Teachers

In order to support the work of teachers and the learning of students, lead learners provide professional learning time and supportive structures so that everyone is engaged in work that makes a difference. Refer to *Transforming Schools and Systems Using Assessment: A*

Practical Guide for ideas regarding time, resources, and professional learning. Assessment *for* learning isn't just for students in classrooms—it's for all of us.

There are three parts to "beginning with the end in mind":

1. "Unpack" all the standards or learning outcomes. Teachers need time to examine and deconstruct the standards or learning outcomes and find ways to understand them more fully before being able to use them as a guide. Knowing the destination isn't enough preparation for a journey—you also need maps to guide you along the way. When teachers unpack the learning destination (see accompanying example in grade 9 English), they come to more fully understand how they can help students achieve the learning. After all, what matters most is not what teachers teach; it is what students learn.

2. Work across departments or grade levels to revisit syllabi, curriculum maps, and the learning pathways. This process helps ensure that teachers are working toward the end, rather than engaging students in an irrelevant collection of activities, assignments, assessment tasks, and tests. We communicate a common vision to students and parents when we collaborate with our colleagues in creating a definition of quality and illustrating it with selected samples of student work. This helps everyone work toward the same goals.

GRADE 9 ENGLISH	
DESTINATION	**EVIDENCE**
Students will, in a consistent, self-directed, and independent manner. . . • Produce quality pieces of writing • Demonstrate understanding of the elements of narrative • Develop English language skills • Effectively communicate ideas and share products with others • Effectively collaborate with peers in the learning process • Collect evidence of learning in a portfolio • Assess the work of self and others in a thoughtful and productive manner	• Writing pieces: autobiographical short stories • Reading responses • Plot diagrams • Video/audio tape of oral storytelling • Illustrations • Journal entries • Self and peer assessments • Large/small group participation • Working independently • Presenting work to others
SAMPLES/MODELS	**EVALUATION**

• Past student writing samples
• Sample videotape of past student oral presentations
• Past student samples of vocabulary notebooks
• In-class modeling of plot diagrams
• Samples of past student reading responses
• Samples of past student journals
	• Produces quality written assignments that:
	  - meet set criteria
	  - show multiple drafts that are edited and revised for content, spelling, grammar, and punctuation (product)
	• Produces reading assignments that:
	  - meet set criteria
	  - show evidence of understanding the reading (product)
	• Consistently reflects upon work and learning in a thoughtful and directed manner (conversation)
	• Works cooperatively and independently in producing and presenting work (observation)

3. Analyze student work together. Looking at student work allows us to come to an understanding of what level of quality is expected, and to recognize possible pathways students might take to achieve success. Analyzing student work also informs our professional judgment and helps us become clearer and more consistent about what we value. As a result, teachers can be more specific and descriptive in their formative assessment, providing learners with more helpful feedback.

Completing the tasks outlined at the end of chapter 3 in *Making Classroom Assessment Work* (shown below) will help your colleagues begin their assessment plan in one subject area with the end—the learning outcomes and standards—in mind.

Guiding Our Own Learning

Begin to draft your own assessment plan by considering the following steps:

1. Choose a subject area and one term to focus on. You may find it easier to begin with one unit of study.

2. Summarize the learning goals (also called learning standards or learning outcomes) into a clear description of the learning destination.

3. Read and review the documents for your subject area and grade level to see if your description is an accurate summary.

4. Check your description with a colleague as well as someone you know who does not work in education. Ask for feedback that focuses on ways to make it clear and simple enough so that others can easily understand the learning destination.

Guiding the Learning of Students

Ask your students to read your draft of one learning destination and tell you what it means. Talk about it. Ask them for suggestions for any changes that will make it more easily understood by them and their parents.

From © 2011 *Making Classroom Assessment Work* (3rd edition) by Anne Davies, p. 32

Being a Lead Learner

As leaders, we also need to walk the talk. This means modeling the very same actions we are asking of classroom teachers in our work as lead teacher. Here are some questions to keep on track to assessment for everyone's learning:

- How do I articulate the district and school vision and mission in language everyone will understand?
- How do I share the description with my learners (students, teachers, staff, parents, community) and explain how it guides my work and the collection of evidence?
- How do I use the description to guide my work with all learners? Do I think through how I can help all learners learn and achieve more, and reach our learning destination?
- How do I guide from the side? Do I show rather than tell? Do I facilitate or present?

We can't change others—only ourselves. Unless we, as lead learners, talk about, demonstrate, and use assessment *for* learning in our own daily work, classroom teachers will be tempted to wait until this "latest new thing" passes. Some of the ways successful leaders are doing this work include modeling, engaging as a lead learner, and providing multiple pathways to success. Here are some examples.

Modeling beginning with the end in mind:

School, district, or division plans are shared in simple, understandable language.

Meetings begin with the learning goals being articulated.

Professional learning is clearly and explicitly linked to school and district goals and to the work of classroom teachers.

School and district plans and budgets make explicit connections to the learning destination for students.

Engaging as a lead teacher:

One superintendent engages trustees in developing ground rules and in setting criteria around committee meetings.

A principal engages faculty in setting criteria by asking: What is important to ensure that this is a successful faculty meeting?

One district's staff supervision and feedback process involves developing a clear description of what success—quality—looks like for each position.

Planning multiple pathways to success:

Teachers are invited to post signs on their classroom door to bring a focus to district personnel observing in classrooms. The signs read, "As you walk through my classroom, please notice we are engaged in assessment *for* learning. You will know this because. . ."

A principal meets with all faculty members and brainstorms a list in response to the question: What does outstanding teaching look like in our school? This is used to guide the supervision and professional growth planning process.

Consider how beginning with the end in mind impacts the learning process. If professional golf operated like most schools, tournaments would begin with all the flags and signposts removed and the following challenge issued: "There are 18 holes. Find them and do it in the right order." Our challenge is to move beyond theory in our practice as leaders and to put guides in place that help learners find their way to the *end*.

Planning to Walk the Talk

Record the end you have in mind for this year. Make a list of what it will look and sound like when you have been successful. Think about what evidence you might have. Consider quantitative and qualitative evidence. List it. How does this fit with the goals inherent in your position? Is there anything missing? If so, add it along with the evidence you would need to prove you've been successful. Place your notes in your draft portfolio collection to reference later.

Describing Success

"Students can assess themselves only when they have a sufficiently clear picture of the targets their learning is meant to attain."

Paul Black and Dylan Wiliam

Contents

"What do you want?" says a student. "How good is good enough?" asks a colleague. "What does excellence look like?" you wonder. These are questions that relate to standards or learning outcomes. Educational guidelines provide a list of learning expectations for each grade level. However, standards often define what students need to learn and be able to do without *showing* what it looks like when they do. For example, "communicates effectively in writing" looks different for a seven-year-old than for a sixteen-year-old. Teachers may know what the standard says but have no idea what quality of success looks like for students they are teaching.

Students have a better chance of being successful if they know what success looks like. For example, we cannot assume that students know what a good presentation or retelling looks like unless they have witnessed one. There is too much room for miscommunication when we use only words. There are many ways to help students understand and recognize success. Teachers can demonstrate, show samples, and co-construct criteria with students to help them understand how success can be achieved.

Sample and Exemplar Collections

Samples and exemplar collections can take many forms, including maps, reading responses, writing projects, mathematical thinking, problem solving, videos of oral presentations, computer animations, or research projects—anything that illustrates what students are expected to know and do in the classroom. Effective samples of student work illustrate the description of learning and answer the question, What will it look like when I've learned it? Using samples to represent the levels of quality involved in meeting standards can serve not only to help students understand the expectations, but also to improve the professional judgments of teachers. Samples or exemplars can be used by teachers when they:

- Develop criteria with students
- Show the range of possible ways to represent their learning (give evidence)
- Assess and give descriptive feedback about student work
- Help others understand more about student learning
- Inform professional judgment

Teachers must be careful in choosing appropriate samples to show students. If samples are limited to showing what students already know and can do, they fail to orient students toward what they need to know next. When samples represent work that is too far away from what students know and are able to do, students may not see how to get from where they are to where they need to be.

Samples help students understand what is possible and what is important. When teachers and students record these ideas on a brainstormed list, they have begun the process of co-constructing criteria. (See page 42 for more information about the four-step process to constructing criteria.)

When samples show a range or variety of acceptable work, they support students to represent what they know in different ways. For example, if the curriculum standard states that a student should be able to "describe the water cycle," they could write about it, draw a labeled diagram, talk about it using props, or even act it out. The standard does not change, but how the students demonstrate their understanding of that standard can be different.

When teachers share samples that illustrate this range of possibilities, the criteria that are set enable them to fairly assess a variety of projects. Students look for what is common among the samples, in order to identify quality and success.

Samples, Criteria, and Descriptive Feedback

Consider the teacher who tries to give students a lot of timely feedback. Over the course of a week, she works hard and manages to give each student specific, descriptive feedback four times.

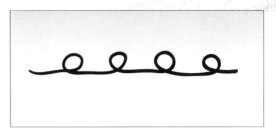

Now imagine the teacher has shared samples with her class and has involved students in co-constructing criteria. Before asking students to turn in their work for feedback, she pauses and asks students to self-assess using the samples or criteria that they have developed together (i.e., give themselves feedback). Without the teacher working any harder, the students receive twice the amount of feedback to feed their learning forward.

Then imagine the classroom is a place where everyone understands quality because they have looked at samples and set criteria and have been using the language of assessment. This time, the teacher asks students to give their work to someone else to assess, using the samples or criteria. Their job is to review the work and find evidence of two things that are the same in the sample or that meet the criteria and to select one thing that needs to be improved.

Next, students are asked to self-assess and give themselves specific, descriptive feedback. The teacher receives the work and gives the students specific, descriptive feedback that also feeds the learning forward.

Now let's go further. What about the classroom where every student has access to email and the web? Could students send their work to people in other places and get even more feedback to forward the learning? Absolutely. Research shows that students seek feedback when it is easily available and when their work can be improved (Davies 2004).

Samples can also help those outside of the classroom understand the learning that is taking place. This is especially true for parents. Samples can communicate, in a very powerful way, the range of student work. Samples help us to respond to the perennial parent question: How is my child doing compared to the other students in the class? We can share samples of the current range of work and where their child's work is in relation to that range. Samples also provide a strong visual to show parents how their child's work compares to what is expected.

Examining student work in comparison to samples or criteria has shown to improve teachers in professional judgment (ARG 2006). Collections of samples that individual teachers believe illustrate the standard or outcome can be gathered by teams of teachers. When teachers analyze these samples, they come to better understanding and to a collective agreement about what constitutes quality.

Being a Leader

Being present in classrooms is an important leadership role. We must strive to understand the importance of what we are observing by asking questions about how samples, models, exemplars, criteria, or rubrics are being used. To determine whether or not they are being used effectively, consider the following indicators:

- In what ways are teachers taking time to consider whether to use samples with students and when to use them?

- How are samples or models supporting the learning in ways that illustrate the learning destination, the qualities of evidence of learning, the criteria for a process or a product, or a visual map using student work to represent development over time?

- How are samples being used to inform professional judgment of quality and of what success looks like? How are all teachers being helped to value the same things when it comes to grading, marking, and reporting?

- How are samples being used with parents and other professionals who are in a supportive role for students to help them understand the learning gap that exists between the evidence of learning the student is producing and what the student needs to produce?

How can we, as leaders, help and support teachers in using samples effectively?

1. One powerful first step is to provide time for teachers to take stock of their own samples and work with colleagues to expand their collection. Consider doing the end-of-chapter tasks from chapter 4 of *Making Classroom Assessment Work*. These are shown below.

Guiding Our Own Learning

With colleagues or on your own, choose one area of focus and collect a range of samples. Remove all identifying features. It is important that students are not able to identify another student's work. You may need to trade samples with a colleague from another school. Or, ask students to create samples just for this purpose.

As you review the samples, make a list of what you see in each sample that is important for students to notice. Later, as students analyze samples, they will often add other important features and ideas to the list.

Guiding the Learning of Students

Ask students to look at the collected samples. You might choose to look at only one or two in the beginning. Record what they think is important. Draw their attention to any features they are missing. Then, ask for suggestions of one or two things that could have been done to improve the quality of the sample. Suggest they use the sample to guide their own work toward quality.

From © 2011 *Making Classroom Assessment Work* (3rd edition) by Anne Davies, p. 44

2. Leaders need to establish structures that support teachers in collaboratively building a wide range of samples and in having the rich conversations that result during this process. For example, teachers can be encouraged to build a collection of samples of student work that show either what development might look like over time or what quality looks like. This helps make the learning destination clear, for both teachers and students. Teachers can collect samples by themselves over time, but the practice is easier and more powerful if done with colleagues.

Here is a six-step process teachers could follow:

1. Find some interested and willing colleagues.
2. Choose a focus for investigation (e.g., journal writing).
3. Collect a range of samples. (Ensure that they are anonymous.)
4. Analyze what is working and what the next teaching steps could be for each sample. (Compare student samples to exemplars provided by provincial or state assessments, if available.)
5. Build a personal collection.
6. Choose another focus and repeat the cycle.

3. We can teach teachers the four-step process (see following page: brainstorm; sort and categorize; make a T-chart; use, revisit, and revise) for involving students in setting criteria for their work. We can model this process by bringing in video clips of teachers at work in classrooms and help teachers brainstorm criteria by having them respond to prompts such as, "What's important about quality classroom assessment?"

Setting and Using Criteria, 2nd Edition (Gregory, Cameron, and Davies 2011) outlines a process for developing criteria with students:

1. Make a brainstormed list.
2. Sort and categorize the list.
3. Make and post a T-chart.
4. Use and revisit and revise.

When using samples to develop criteria, students first examine the samples and list the important features. The teacher records their ideas on a brainstormed list and may also add to the list. Once the list is complete, the ideas are sorted and transcribed onto a T-chart that can be posted in the class. The list of criteria is then used to help students self-assess, to give descriptive feedback, and to assess student work.

4. We can lead a process that promotes dialogue with teachers about what the samples show in relation to criteria or to the standards. By analyzing samples, teachers examine a broad range of student work, understand better what students are to know, develop a commonly held sense of what learning might look like for students over time, and begin to develop a common language to use with students (see sample on page 47).

Some jurisdictions (such as New Zealand) have collected a vast range of exemplars for different subject areas. These samples can be used in a variety of ways by classroom teachers to:

- Co-construct criteria for different kinds of evidence of learning with students
- Provide better quality feedback
- Help others understand learning
- Increase the accuracy of their professional judgment

After analyzing large numbers of writing samples, a committee developed a description of writing development from K to 12. In order to help teachers understand the description, the committee collected samples from across the jurisdiction to illustrate what students know and are able to do at different grade levels—development over time, from kindergarten to graduation—and the range of development that could be expected at different ages.

5. We can introduce teachers to the practice of using protocols to examine student work. Protocols are valuable resources and professional learning tools that can help teachers learn how to look at and use work samples with students and with each other. Leaders can designate and protect time for teachers to work together. We can share video clips of classrooms where students are reflecting on their own work compared to criteria. We can reallocate time and invite all faculty members to share their use of samples with others. Catherine Glaude (2005, 2010) worked to develop a variety of protocols to support different learning purposes (see sample on next page).

This protocol
can be found as
a reproducible
on page 165 of
appendix 2.

Protocol: Examining Student Work in Relation to Descriptions of Quality

Facilitator: Ensures group sets ground rules and that time limits are strictly observed. Facilitator observes but does not participate.

Prior Preparation: Presenting teacher (PT) has comprehensive collection of student evidence for one term for one child and a description of success for report card symbol that includes qualitative data as well as quantitative data. Participants (Part) have professional expertise—an understanding of the standards or learning outcomes as well as experience teaching children in this age range.

(PT) 10 minutes: Presenting teacher shows comprehensive collection of student evidence for one term, talks about standards, shares the description, but does not talk about the child. When finished, the presenting teacher moves his/her chair back from the group and begins to take notes.

(Part) 15 minutes: Participants describe what they see in the work. What do they notice? What questions do they have? (PT does not respond at this time.)

(Part) 15 minutes: Participants identify the standards they see being evidenced by the collection of work, score the work using the description of a letter grade provided by the presenting teacher, and provide reasons for the score. (PT does not respond at this time.)

(PT) 10 minutes: Presenting teacher rejoins the group. Group members listen to presenting teacher describe the collection of student work more fully, respond to questions, and add information.

(Part) 10 minutes: Participants discuss the implications for assessment, evaluation, and instruction.

(All) 7 minutes: Everyone mentally steps back, reflects, records their thoughts regarding this protocol (in writing, silently), and then shares their thoughts verbally.

PT: Presenting Teacher
Part: Participants

Adapted with permission from *Protocols for Professional Learning Conversations* by Catherine Glaude (2011).

Being a Lead Learner

As lead learners, we also need to walk the talk with regards to describing success. Here are some questions to keep on track with assessment *for* everyone's learning:

- In what ways do I use samples or models to illustrate the learning destination with adult learners?

- In what ways do I engage colleagues, for whom I am a lead learner, in professional learning conversations to describe what an ideal school or district initiative looks like? Do I search out models or samples to inform the conversation?

- As a member of a leadership team, in what ways do I bring forward examples of my work and enter into a dialogue with my colleagues, regarding my working definitions of quality? For example, do we value the same attributes in our teacher and our employee evaluations?

Some of the ways lead learners are doing this work include modeling and engaging in their own assessment *for* learning, and using protocols to improve their understanding of quality leadership.

When leading the way for others, use samples and models such as video clips, text, or live demonstrations. Consider using assessment *for* learning strategies, such as involving adult learners in setting criteria, as a part of faculty meetings. Use more than words to help people picture success; for example, showing plans from other schools can inspire the development of a new program. Model a variety of ways to be informed by qualitative and quantitative data, such as shown in the following examples:

> A school staff engaged in setting criteria for what student engagement and assessment *for* learning would look like in a classroom setting. Three times in the year, the staff divided itself into groups of four or five. These groups walked around the school and through classrooms noting evidence to connect to the criteria they had established. Group members took pictures, made anecdotal notes, collected work samples, and talked to students. This proof was shared at the next faculty meeting, linking it to the criteria it supported.

A superintendent kept a portfolio for trustees as a model for principals who were being asked to show evidence of their growth as leaders.

A principal imitated her superintendent's method of posting the school district's plans and reviewing them at each monthly meeting, noting accomplishments with a highlighter. The result was that the staff maintained a central focus on goals and progress in their ongoing work, ensuring that the school goals would not be forgotten during the busy year.

A superintendent shared her professional growth plan with all administrators to model the format, content, and process of this districtwide expectation.

As a leadership group, we can use protocols for team projects, such as planning school improvements, increasing teacher effectiveness, publishing school newsletters, learning how to work with parents, and so on, so that we experience the development of common understanding of quality and success. Experiencing this process as a participant helps inform our work as a lead learner. Also, when we come to agreement, the district is more likely to be unified and able to use assessment *for* learning to fuel our work toward our vision and mission.

In summary, it is important for us as lead learners to use samples and exemplars to illustrate quality, to support learning, and to continue to acknowledge that students, young and old, learn in different ways and at different rates. Leaders and teachers are making sense of standards by talking with colleagues about samples and the assessment *for* learning process. Our job as leaders is to be thoughtful and curious about how to use assessment *for* learning strategies with adult learners throughout the school system.

Ways to Come to Common Agreement About Quality

Purpose: To engage all participants and resource people in discussing and determining quality level work.

Prior to the Conversation: The professional learning team identifies an area of quality work upon which to focus. Each participant brings two or three samples of student work, of which at least one is determined to be at grade level. All student names are removed or covered, and work is labeled with a number such as 1, 2, or 3. Copies of the work are made for everyone. If student work is lengthy, the work and the focus question may be given ahead of time. The presenting educator identifies a focus question for the feedback: Would you agree this is at-grade-level work? The presenting educator completes a written assessment before beginning the critique (see Preparatory Self-Assessment below) and prepares a five-minute overview of the work.

Time Needed: 30–35 minutes for each review.

1. **Getting Started:** Select a facilitator and a timekeeper. Review the purpose of the protocol and ground rules for this process.

2. **Describing the Context:** The presenting teacher offers any background information and the purpose for the assessment. The focus question is written on chart paper or the board for all to see.

3. **Seeking Understanding:** Three reviewers ask questions to clarify. (3 minutes)

4. **Reviewing the Work:** Group members review the work. They discuss where the work is of quality in terms of the criteria used by students, what could improve the work, and possible next learning and teaching steps for each student. (8 minutes)

5. **Extending the Connections:** The presenting teacher joins the conversation and directs it to any intriguing ideas or points to pursue. (3 minutes)

6. **Summarizing the Ideas:** Each participant has a last word to sum up the conversation. (5 minutes)

7. **Reflecting on the Conversation:** Presenter(s) of the work and reviewers comment briefly on the effectiveness of the protocol. (3 minutes)

8. **Continuing the Learning:** Repeat for each work presented.

Preparatory Self-Assessment:
- The learning purpose that students were given for this work was:
- The learning context for this work was:
- The criteria for success for this work was:
- I assess these samples as being of grade-level quality because:
- In order to improve the quality of these samples, students would need to show evidence or be able to do:
- I think the next learning steps for these students are:

Adapted with permission from *Protocols for Professional Learning Conversations* by Catherine Glaude (2011).

Planning to Walk the Talk

Spend some time collecting samples to use in your work. As you do so, pay attention to what is easy, what is difficult, and what is simply puzzling. These ideas sound simple but require thought and time to implement. The process will not only help you in your work, but will also give you a better understanding of what you are asking your adult learners to do. Consider placing samples that you might use in your draft portfolio collection.

Evidence of Learning

" Only if we expand and reformulate our view of what counts as human intellect will we be able to devise more appropriate ways of assessing it and more effective ways of educating it. "

Howard Gardner

Contents

Once teachers have described what students need to learn and have developed a sense of what success might look like for their students, it is time for them to consider what kinds of evidence of learning they will need to collect. This helps teachers to plan ongoing instruction and ensure validity and reliability. That way, when teachers evaluate at the end of the learning period, they and others can have confidence that they will be able to make high-quality professional judgments and base their teaching on evidence of student learning needs.

Different teachers collect different kinds of evidence, even though the description of what their students need to learn may be the same. This is because the learning experiences that teachers design for different groups of learners may vary. Also, since students learn in different ways and at different times, collections of evidence may vary slightly in terms of how students choose to represent their learning. When making lists of the evidence to collect, teachers need to make sure they plan to gather evidence from a variety of sources and that they gather evidence over time.

Sources of Evidence

There are three general sources of assessment evidence gathered in classrooms: *observations* of learning, *products* students create, and *conversations*—discussing learning with students (BC Ministry of Education 1990, 2000). When evidence is collected from three different sources over time, trends and patterns become apparent, and the reliability and validity of classroom assessment is increased. This process is called *triangulation* (Lincoln and Guba 1984).

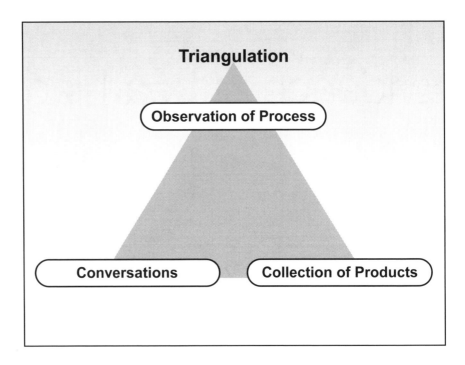

Triangulation

Observation of Process

Conversations   Collection of Products

Reliability: Think "repeatability"—reliability refers to students producing the same kind of result at different times.

Validity: Think "valid"—the extent to which the evidence from multiple sources matches the quality levels expected in light of the standards or learning outcomes.

Observing the Learning

The list of evidence teachers plan to collect needs to include the observations they will make while students are learning. The record of observations becomes evidence.

Teachers might observe: formal and informal presentations, drama presentations, applications of the scientific method, music-related activities, read-alouds, group or partner activities, discussions about students' work, plans and designs for a Web page, acts of persuading and giving opinions, abilities to follow and give instructions, acts of listening, arguments, predictions, measurements, charades, dances, communication in small-group settings, conflict resolutions, feedback, partner or team work, identification of sounds, rhythm games, cartooning, playing instruments, jigsaws, demonstrations, skills development, movement exercises, keyboarding, gestures, pantomimes, reenactments, gymnastic routines, sign language, graphic designs, simulations, debates, answers to questions, presentations of work, songs, verbalizations of abstract reasoning, sculptures, choral readings, conversations, dialogues, dramatic readings, oral descriptions, oral reports, puppet shows, Readers' Theatre activities, storytelling, demonstrations of symbolic thinking, lesson instruction, slide show creations, role plays, verbal explanations, and verbal instructions. This list could include anything a teacher might observe students doing or might ask them to do. See the following sample of Criteria for Problem Solving and the corresponding observation record form.

Observations are essential if classroom assessment and evaluation are to be reliable and valid. In addition to being necessary for triangulating the evidence of learning, some learning can only be observed. For example, some students are better able to show what they know by doing it. These "in action" kinds of learners and younger children, who may be able to record little in writing, need some of their learning assessed through observation. Also, products "under construction" can provide teachers with opportunities to observe students' learning. Without enough observational evidence, evaluations at reporting time are at risk of being invalid.

Criteria for Problem Solving

Strategy
(Decide the strategy you will use to solve the problem.)

Organize the information
(What information am I going to need and how will I organize it?)

Label your work
(Example: 67 pounds or 23 seconds.)

Verify
(Look back at the problem and make sure your answer works.)

Explain
(Explain your thinking and how you got your answer.)

Math Problem Solving

Teacher_____ Grade _____

NAMES	/	/	/	/	/	/	/
RAHIM	SOLVE	SOLVE	SOLVE	SOLVE	SOLVE	SOLVE	SOLVE
OSA	SOLVE	SOLVE	SOLVE	SOLVE	SOLVE	SOLVE	SOLVE
ALEXI	SOLVE	SOLVE	SOLVE	SOLVE	SOLVE	SOLVE	SOLVE
ISAAC	SOLVE	SOLVE	SOLVE	SOLVE	SOLVE	SOLVE	SOLVE
JADE	SOLVE	SOLVE	SOLVE	SOLVE	SOLVE	SOLVE	SOLVE
TANIKA	SOLVE	SOLVE	SOLVE	SOLVE	SOLVE	SOLVE	SOLVE
KAYLA	SOLVE	SOLVE	SOLVE	SOLVE	SOLVE	SOLVE	SOLVE
HOLLY	SOLVE	SOLVE	SOLVE	SOLVE	SOLVE	SOLVE	SOLVE
DAKOTA	SOLVE	SOLVE	SOLVE	SOLVE	SOLVE	SOLVE	SOLVE

Collecting Products

Teachers collect various kinds of evidence to show what students can do. These include projects, assignments, notebooks, and tests. As teachers become more knowledgeable about the implications of different theories of intelligence (Gardner 1984; Levine 1993; Sternberg 1996), they are expanding the ways students show or represent what they know. For example, when students are asked to represent what they know only in writing, some will be unable, due to their lack of skill as writers. However, when asked to demonstrate the process in action or to give an oral presentation, their knowledge and skill may rapidly become apparent.

More and more teachers are introducing an element of choice into the ways students show their learning. Some teachers create a list of ideas with students (see accompanying figure). Over time, the list can grow as students learn more about different ways of representing their learning.

Different ways to show what we know...

- draw a diagram
- make a time line
- make a poster
- write a story
- do an oral presentation
- write a poem
- build a model
- design a Web page
- create a puzzle
- make a video
- create an iMovie
- make a podcast
- make a recording
- design a T-shirt
- do a report
- write a song
- create a collage
- build a diorama
- write a play
- do a journal entry
- perform a puppet show
- input e-journal entry

Conversations About Learning

Conversations about learning involve listening to what students have to say about their learning or reading what they record about their learning. The conversation may be face-to-face or in writing.

Teachers listen to learners during class meetings, at individual or group conferences, or when they read students' self-assessments about their work. Teachers also have opportunities to listen when students assess their work in relation to criteria, analyze their work samples for their portfolios, or prepare to report to parents about their learning.

When teachers listen to students in these ways, they invite them to think about their learning. As students think and explain, teachers can gather evidence about what they know and understand. Teachers can find out about what students found to be, for example, difficult or easy, what they might do differently next time, or what risks they are taking as learners. Students learn more when teachers take the time to involve them in self-assessment (Black and Wiliam 1998; Young 2000). The ability to articulate their learning processes—as part of a reader's response, a mathematics response, or in some other way—has become an increasingly important aspect of classroom and external assessment.

Creating a Plan

It takes some planning for teachers to make sure they have enough evidence, the right kind of evidence, and evidence that is reliable and valid. They have a better chance of collecting reliable and valid evidence of learning when they ensure they have proof of learning from multiple sources collected over time. Teachers also plan to collect a range of evidence—both qualitative and quantitative data—matching it to the curriculum standards for which they are responsible. They look at the learning destination and match it to the evidence asking: Are there any gaps? Are there any overlaps? Am I collecting evidence from multiple sources?

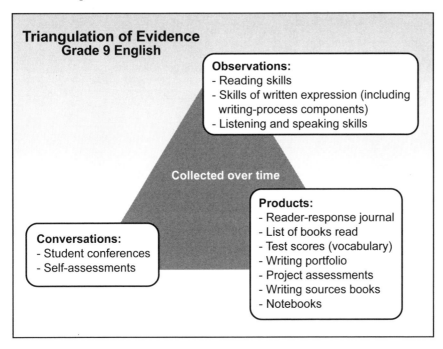

Triangulation of Evidence
Grade 9 English

Observations:
- Reading skills
- Skills of written expression (including writing-process components)
- Listening and speaking skills

Collected over time

Products:
- Reader-response journal
- List of books read
- Test scores (vocabulary)
- Writing portfolio
- Project assessments
- Writing sources books
- Notebooks

Conversations:
- Student conferences
- Self-assessments

It is important that teachers use the evidence available for each student and compare it to the same set of curriculum standards and expectations. In a standards-based evaluation system, teachers have to account for each student's learning in relation to the expectations for that grade and subject area unless an individual education plan is in place for a learner with special needs. While a teacher's written and verbal comments may speak to the amount of progress students have made in their learning, the evaluation must reflect their accomplishments in relation to the standards for the subject area and level at which they are working.

" I can't say enough about how impressed I am by how specific and articulate my students have become as a result of setting criteria, doing reflections, and keeping learning goals portfolios."

Holly Tornrose,
High School English Teacher

Being a Leader

Indicators of Classroom Application

When teachers begin with the end in mind, they have a plan for collecting evidence—one that has been developed in relation to the standards or learning outcomes, and for *all* standards being evaluated. Evidence of learning is comprehensive and includes both qualitative and quantitative data from at least three different sources: products, observations of process, and conversations with students (verbally or in writing). It is important that the evidence of learning is collected over time, so that patterns and trends can be discerned.

Some questions to consider asking classroom teachers:

- How will the evidence you are planning to collect show whether or not students have learned what they needed to learn?
- Is there any unnecessary evidence you are collecting that is not directly related to any required standard?
- How are you collecting evidence from multiple sources?
- How are you collecting enough evidence to see patterns over time?
- Are you collecting too much evidence? Is there anything you can stop collecting?
- How are your students involved in collecting and organizing the evidence?
- When you prepare for evaluation, how are you going to value the evidence of learning you have collected from multiple sources over time?
- How are you clearly communicating the evaluation process and the evidence of learning being valued and evaluated to students and their parents?

Supporting Classroom Teachers

Lead learners support classroom teachers when they provide time and guidance so that teachers can develop their own plans, work with colleagues to polish their plans for collecting evidence, and review the body of evidence in preparation for reporting. Engaging teachers in developing plans for collecting evidence of learning helps them develop the expertise and confidence to make sound professional judgments during the learning, as well as in evaluating reports. Consider providing time for teachers to complete the following tasks from the end of chapter 5 in *Making Classroom Assessment Work*.

Guiding Our Own Learning

Develop a plan for collecting evidence by returning to your earlier description of what students need to learn, be able to do, and be able to articulate (see "Guiding Our Own Learning" from chapter 3, page 32).

Think about the evidence you and your students will be able to collect. Consider observations, products, and conversations. Make a list of all the evidence related to the learning destination.

When you are finished, review the list, asking yourself:
- Will my evidence show whether or not students have learned what they needed to learn?
- Is there any evidence I am collecting for which I am not accountable?
- Am I collecting evidence from multiple sources?
- Am I collecting enough evidence to see patterns over time?
- Am I collecting too much evidence? Is there anything I can stop collecting?
- How can my students be involved in collecting and organizing the evidence?

Show your draft to a trusted colleague. Ask if he or she thinks there is anything you have missed or anything you could delete. Consider the suggestions and make your own decision.

When we divide up the responsibility for developing the first draft, everyone benefits—we improve our work and have more confidence in it. Talk about your list of evidence with others. Share your list. Invite others to share their work with you. After you have piloted the process with one subject area, proceed to do the same with other subject areas or courses.

Guiding the Learning of Students

Prepare the students to *assess their way to success* by asking them to identify all the evidence they might have that shows proof of meeting the learning destination. Ask them to consider not only what *you* would need for proof but also what *others* (i.e., parents, employers, other institutions) would need for proof. Make a joint list of all the possible ideas for evidence of learning in relation to the learning destination. Remind them that the evidence is only a record of what they have learned; it isn't—and can never be—the whole story.

From © 2011 *Making Classroom Assessment Work* (3rd edition) by Anne Davies, p. 54

Continue the work as a faculty through one or more of the following ideas:

- Guide classroom teachers in developing a plan for collecting evidence in relation to the standards their students must meet. Provide time and a structure for them to work with each other in order to polish their evidence collection.
- Ask teachers to submit their draft evidence plan, as part of their curriculum overview, for the upcoming term.
- Work with teachers to help them identify common sources of assessment evidence across their classes. Encourage them to go beyond simple tests and to collect evidence from three different sources; for example, they might use a performance task wherein students are observed applying their learning and then asked to articulate what they did and why. Provide time and a structure for teachers to meet, analyze this triangulated student evidence, and learn more about quality work, as well as about effective teaching and learning strategies.
- Prior to reporting, ask teachers to take turns submitting the complete body of evidence (products, observations, and conversations) for one student in one class. This will be reviewed by their colleagues and principals, and instructive feedback will be offered.

Research Connection:

Pencil-and-paper tests and tasks are not objective measures of student learning. These kinds of assessments can indicate certain information when used properly, but cannot be used to measure all important knowledge, abilities, and skills (Stiggins 2004; Harlen 2006).

Being a Lead Learner

Being a lead learner is challenging because we must be trailblazers for others. Adult learners are more willing to try a new concept when they witness our struggle to master it. We are better equipped to anticipate problem areas that they might encounter and to appreciate their frustrations and accomplishments when we have walked the path ourselves.

One way to model triangulation at the district level is to examine the process by which school-based administrators are selected. Consider the following questions:

- What evidence are you collecting to indicate that an individual is prepared for the leadership role?
- Does this evidence come from a variety of sources?

Here are two examples of ways that leaders can model this assessment *for* learning technique:

One district uses a selection process based on triangulation of evidence that is outlined in the figure on the facing page.

In another district, the first interviews that take place are student interviews of all the candidates (teachers, school administrators, and district administrators). Leaders select students that will reflect the diversity of the student population to be involved in the interview process. These students are assisted to brainstorm a variety of questions so they can feel confident as they enter the process. During the interviews, the adult facilitator observes, but says as little as possible.

District Administration Evidence Collection

Product:
- Résumé
- In-basket assignment
- Statement of educational philosophy
- Presentation about leadership beliefs

Conversation:
- Informal conference to better get to know the candidate
- Formal conversation or interview with some topics presented to the candidate prior to the appointment

Observation:
- Observation of applicant as he or she teaches a class
- Observation of applicant as he or she chairs a committee meeting
- Observation of applicant as he or she interacts with a parent group

Planning to Walk the Talk

Consider applying these ideas in your leadership role:

- Develop your own plan, with data being collected from at least three different sources over time, so you can look for patterns and trends. You might do this as you collect evidence of effective teaching and learning in classrooms or for the school or district growth plan.
- Consider using triangulation of data (products, observations, and conversations) to inform your selection process of teachers and administrators, supervision of teacher performance, as well as assessment of ongoing implementation of district priorities, such as districtwide professional learning plans.
- As a model for your colleagues, provide evidence of learning by sharing your professional growth portfolio.

- Invite a few colleagues to work with you to improve the collection of evidence in relation to teacher practice. Using the protocol in this chapter, examine one collection of evidence for an anonymous teacher whom you are evaluating. Consider strengths, areas needing improvement, and one goal area, as well as how *you* might improve *your* evidence collection to better support teacher growth and development. This process will help you understand how the protocol engages participants, while enabling your professional judgment.

Place your work in your draft portfolio collection.

Involving Students in Classroom Assessment

Contents

"Good assessment tasks are interchangeable with good instructional tasks.""

Lorrie Shepard

If we want engaged, enthusiastic learners who strive to produce quality work while learning and achieving more, then we need to involve students in the classroom assessment process. The research is clear. When teachers use assessment *in support of* learning, students become more engaged in learning. Teachers are finding that six key assessment *for* learning processes help to create classrooms where learning is the number-one focus:

1. Involve students in co-constructing criteria.
2. Engage students in self-assessment.
3. Increase the sources of specific, descriptive feedback.
4. Assist students to set goals.
5. Have students collect evidence of learning in relation to standards.
6. Have students present evidence of learning in relation to standards.

Involve Students in Co-Constructing Criteria

When teachers ask students what is important in creating a map, writing a story, doing a research report, or presenting to a small group, students get a chance to share their ideas. When teachers involve students in setting criteria in relation to any important product, process, or collection of evidence of learning, they learn more about what the students know, and students come to understand what is important while they learn. Refer to Gregory et al.'s (2011) four-step process for setting and using criteria on page 42.

1. Brainstorm a list of ideas.

WHAT IS IMPORTANT FOR A QUALITY REPORT & POSTER?

- MAKES SENSE
- HAS BEGINNING, MIDDLE, & END
- NEAT
- INTERESTING INFORMATION
- USE PARAGRAPHS
- INDENT
- USE DESCRIPTIVE LANGUAGE
- PUNCTUATE
- CAPITALS
- SPELLING
- ADD HUMOR, DRAMA, EMOTION
- PRACTICE READING IT OUT LOUD
- GRAB THE READER'S ATTENTION
- ADD DETAILS
- REMEMBER YOUR AUDIENCE

2. Sort and group the ideas.

WHAT IS IMPORTANT FOR A QUALITY REPORT & POSTER?

- ☆ MAKES SENSE
- ☆ HAS BEGINNING, MIDDLE, & END
- ☆ NEAT
- INTERESTING INFORMATION
- USE PARAGRAPHS
- INDENT
- USE DESCRIPTIVE LANGUAGE
- PUNCTUATE
- CAPITALS
- ☆ SPELLING
- ADD HUMOR, DRAMA, EMOTION
- ☆ PRACTICE READING IT OUT LOUD
- GRAB THE READER'S ATTENTION
- ADD DETAILS
- REMEMBER YOUR AUDIENCE

3. Make and post a T-chart.

CRITERIA FOR A BOOK REPORT & POSTER	SPECIFICS / DETAILS
INTERESTING TO AUDIENCE	- INTERESTING INFORMATION - USE DESCRIPTIVE LANGUAGE - ADD HUMOR, DRAMA, EMOTION - PRACTICE READING IT OUT LOUD - GRAB THE READER'S ATTENTION - ADD DETAILS - REMEMBER YOUR AUDIENCE
EASY TO FOLLOW	- MAKES SENSE - HAS BEGINNING, MIDDLE, & END - USE PARAGRAPHS - SPELLING - PRACTICE READING IT OUT LOUD - NEAT
EASY TO READ	- NEAT - INDENT PARAGRAPHS - PUNCTUATE (,."*?! ETC) - CAPITALS - SPELLING - REMEMBER YOUR AUDIENCE

4. Use and revise as you learn more.

CRITERIA FOR A BOOK REPORT & POSTER	SPECIFICS / DETAILS
INTERESTING TO AUDIENCE	- INTERESTING INFORMATION - USE DESCRIPTIVE LANGUAGE - ADD HUMOR, DRAMA, EMOTION - PRACTICE READING IT OUT LOUD - GRAB THE READER'S ATTENTION - ADD DETAILS - REMEMBER YOUR AUDIENCE - COLOR HELPS AUDIENCE SEE WHAT IS IMPORTANT
EASY TO FOLLOW	- MAKES SENSE - HAS BEGINNING, MIDDLE, & END - USE PARAGRAPHS - SPELLING - PRACTICE READING IT OUT LOUD - NEAT - POSTER NEEDS TO LINK WORDS
EASY TO READ	- NEAT - INDENT PARAGRAPHS - PUNCTUATE (,."*?! ETC) - CAPITALS - SPELLING - REMEMBER YOUR AUDIENCE - PRINT BIG ENOUGH FOR PEOPLE TO SEE / USE LARGE FONT

Engage Students in Self-Assessment

Self-assessment provides time for students to process and learn. When teachers engage students in self-assessment, they give them time to:

- Process—to learn—during teaching time
- Give themselves feedback
- Transition from one activity or class to another

Frequent self-assessment ensures the focus stays on learning. The result is that teachers have an opportunity to find out what students are thinking and the kinds of understandings that are developing. It also allows teachers to listen to students and to use their ideas as starting points for lessons. Self-assessment teaches students how to self-monitor, especially when it is informed by clear criteria and samples or models. Students who self-monitor are developing and practicing the skills needed to be lifelong, independent learners.

Self-assessment can be a valuable source of evidence since, when it is attached to student work, it provides a place for a student's voice to be heard. For example, students can explain, as a part of their self-assessments, why a particular piece of evidence is worth attending to as evidence of learning on the way toward the learning destination.

Increase the Sources of Specific, Descriptive Feedback

The more specific, descriptive feedback students receive while they are learning, the more learning is possible. Teachers who want all students to succeed arrange ways for students to give themselves feedback or receive feedback from others. Teachers do this by involving students in co-constructing criteria so they can give themselves feedback in relation to the criteria as they are working and learning. When teachers impose the criteria, no matter how clear, it is not as effective as when students help set the criteria in their own words.

A second way teachers increase the feedback possibilities for students is to provide models, samples, or exemplars; analyze their key attributes *with* students to show what success looks like; and then ask students to use the samples, models, and exemplars to help them reach quality. Sometimes teachers demonstrate a range of quality by providing samples that show what the journey to quality looks like; other times teachers show only the best exemplars—samples that illustrate quality. The decision as to whether to show a range of samples or only high-quality samples depends on the teacher's purpose for using samples.

Your Name: _____
Today's Date: _____

Bless Me, Ultima Presentation
Self-Reflection

Respond to the following in a few sentences.

1. What was one strength of the way in which you presented your poster project (this could be one of the criteria your group focused on or another quality of a good oral presentation)?

I thought my voice was very clear and loud. This is important in making a good presentation because people have to be able to hear you when you make a presentation.

2. What is an area in which you think you need to improve during your next oral presentation review (this could be one of the criteria your group focused on or another quality of a good oral presentation)?

I think I should make better visuals because it shows how good it is.

3. What could you do in preparation to practice or develop this skill?

Practice drawing.

With thanks to Holly Tornrose, Maine

A third way teachers are arranging for students to receive more specific, descriptive feedback is by asking students themselves, peers, and parents to assess work in relation to criteria and models (see accompanying figures). The quality of peer assessment increases when it is based on clear criteria and appropriate samples. This not only increases the amount and rate of students' learning, but can also reduce teachers' time spent grading student work.

Portfolio Review

Date of Review _____

Name of Reviewer _____

Two Stars

YOU READ BETTER ALL THE TIME. I LIKE YOUR PATTERNS.

YOU SURE KNOW A LOT ABOUT BONES. WONDERFUL DRAWING.

One Wish

TO KEEP LEARNING AND ENJOYING SCHOOL.

Adapted from *Conferencing and Reporting* (2nd edition) by Gregory, Cameron, and Davies, p. 63.

Help Students Set Goals

Csikszentmihalyi's (1993) research led him to write, "Flow usually occurs when there are clear goals a person tries to reach, and when there is unambiguous feedback as to how well he or she is doing" (p. 179). Brain research is also indicating that closing in on a goal triggers a part of the brain linked to motivation. Whether you consider the often-reported study where students who recorded their goals in writing were far more likely to achieve them or studies related to fitness, weight-loss programs, or changing any habit, the trend is clearly in support of the power of goal setting. Goals help bring focus and energy to bear in the service of learning. Teachers working with students know that goals become more specific and realistic when there are clear criteria and samples that show what success looks like (see figures on following page). Goals may be short term, in that they identify next steps in the learning, or long-term, i.e., focused on improving the quality of the work—the evidence of learning—over a term or year.

Goal Setting
Grade 6

Subject area: _Spelling_ Teacher: _____

Goal: _improve spelling in daily work_
90% accuracy in all written work

Evidence: _show my journals_
written work in all subject areas

Subject area: _Reading_ Teacher: _____

Goal: _Read 4 books this year_

Evidence: _Make a report for each book_

Subject area: _Computer_ Teacher: _H_

Goal: _Type 34 words in a minute_
Mavis Beacon

Evidence: _print out typing scores_

HOW DID I DO?
WHAT COUNTS AT SOCCER?

NEEDS ATTENTION

WORKING AT IT

RIGHT ON

GOAL: _I was pushing. I need_
to stop pushing and use words
NAME: _____

With thanks to Lisa McCluskey, Alberta

Have Students Collect Evidence of Learning

Purpose is paramount. When students understand they have a responsibility to collect evidence of learning in relation to the learning destination, they have a purpose. As a result, the important work of collecting evidence of their learning is more likely to be engaging and relevant. Also, when students know what they are to learn and what it looks like to be successful, they are informed enough to self-monitor their way to success. When students collect, reflect, organize, and present evidence of learning to others, they acquire skills to be more accountable for their own learning. Teachers may invite students to collect their evidence in any number of ways, from online collections to physical portfolios with a specific structure. Again, when the learning destination is clear and students have played a role in brainstorming possible evidence, they are more likely to know what needs to be collected in order for them to show proof of their learning.

Have Students Present Evidence of Learning

Audience is key to any presentation. Today's students have a variety of audiences: in their homes, in their communities, and online. As schools seek to be more accountable to the larger community, students are presenting their evidence of learning to a more diverse range of people, both face-to-face and online. Students who learn to present themselves as learners are more prepared to keep families and community informed and involved. Students who know they will be providing proof of learning often assume more responsibility for collecting, reflecting, and organizing the evidence (see figures below and on following page). They are aware of what they know and can present their evidence of learning in ways appropriate to the audience, whether it is made up of their teacher(s), parents, peers, or other community members.

This Is an Example of What I Am Reading

I'm a Good Reader because:

☆ I read real slow so I can understand.
☆ I give my own opinion.
☆ I flip through the first 2 pages.

Book Title: The Cricket
Author: George Selden

Bring a book.

Read the book.

On your own.

Write.

The Cricket in Times Square

Mario slipped out of the newsstand and stood waiting. The next time he heard the sound, he went toward it. It seemed to come from one corner, next to the stairs that led up to Forty-second Street. Softly, Mario went toward the spot. For several seconds there was only the whispering silence. Whatever it was that was making the sound had heard him coming and was quiet. Silently Mario waited. Then he heard it again, rising from a pile of waste papers and soot that had blown against the concrete wall.

He went down and very gently began to lift off the papers. One by one he inspected them and laid them to one side. Down near the bottom the papers became dirtier and dirtier. Mario reached the floor. He began to feel with his hands through the dust and soot. And wedged in a crack under all the refuse, he found what he was looking for.

It was a little insect, about an inch long, and covered with dirt. It had six legs, two long antennae on its head and what seemed to be a pair of wings folded on its back. Holding his discovery as carefully as his fingers could, Mario lifted the insect up and rested him in the palm of his hand.

"A cricket!" he exclaimed.

Keeping his cupped hand very steady, Mario walked back to the newsstand. The cricket didn't move. And he didn't make that little musical noise anymore.

Signed: _____
Date: _____

PROGRESSFOLIO

PRODUCED BY: _____

TABLE OF CONTENTS

I. CONTENT KNOWLEDGE: Samples in this pocket will show what students' factual knowledge is in the content area(s).

II. INQUIRY AND PROBLEM SOLVING (REASONING): Samples in this pocket will show students' ability to apply knowledge and skills in new situations.

III. SKILLS AND TECHNOLOGY: Samples in this pocket will show ability to perform certain skills in the subject and apply use of technology.

IV. OBSERVATIONS: Samples in this pocket will be formal observation pieces by the teachers, peers, and self-observations.

V. IMPROVEMENT: Samples in this pocket will show improvement over time in the class.

VI. TOGETHER (GROUPWORK): Samples in this pocket will be pieces students have worked on with others.

VII. FAVORITE: Samples in this pocket will be the student's favorite products or activities in the class.

VIII. PICTURE THIS/FEEDBACK FORMS: Samples in this pocket will be pictures of the student in action in the class as well as feedback and self evaluation forms.

Quote:

"We can tell a little more of a truth. In doing so, it turns out that we can avoid pretending that a student's whole performance or intelligence can be summed up in one number." —Peter Elbow

With thanks to Misty McBriety, Maine

Thank you for coming this afternoon. It would be wonderful if you could leave your special child with two compliments and a suggestion on how to improve.

Dear: _____

Today I really liked:

1. _____

2. _____

One way to improve:

_____

_____
Signature

Being a Leader

Indicators of Classroom Application

As you visit and observe in classrooms, consider the following questions that indicate whether students are being involved in assessment *for* learning:

1. How are students involved in co-constructing criteria for any products, processes, or collections of evidence of learning? Is there evidence that criteria-building has been shared?

2. When you examine rubrics, are they supportive of all students' learning? For example, do the different levels help students understand what they need to do differently in order to achieve more success or do they merely point out errors? How can you help teachers revisit and refine rubrics so they support all learners?

3. How are students engaged in self-assessment? When you ask students to give evidence that they are learning, can they be specific? Do they use the language of shared criteria?

4. What sources of feedback do students access? Are students able to be involved in peer assessment? Is the feedback specific and descriptive?

5. How do students set goals and collect evidence to show they are working toward their goals? Are the goals students set both relevant and realistic? How are teachers planning to involve students in collecting evidence in relation to goals and then, if needed, revising the goals for the next learning?

6. How are students collecting evidence of learning in relation to standards or learning outcomes?

7. How are students presenting evidence of learning in relation to standards or learning outcomes?

Supporting Classroom Teachers

In order to assist teachers to think through ways to involve students more deeply in the assessment process, consider providing time for them to read chapter 6 in *Making Classroom Assessment Work* and then invite them to work together to complete the end of chapter tasks (shown below).

Guiding Our Own Learning

Think about assessment in your classroom. How does it guide instruction? How do you involve students in the process? What do you do that is similar to the ideas you have read in this chapter? What is different? Record your thoughts.

Consider meeting with your learning circle to share ideas and strategies that work. Learning circles often find it helpful to focus on ideas related to the following topics: involving students in setting criteria, collecting samples, engaging students in peer and self-assessment, and finding ways to collect and organize evidence, as well as ways to have students share evidence of their learning with others.

Guiding the Learning of Students

As you prepare students to assess their way to success, remember students need practice setting criteria, engaging in peer and self-assessment, and collecting and organizing evidence of their learning, as well as sharing evidence of their learning with others. Identify a starting point for you and your students. Consider co-constructing criteria around a project, a process, or a simple classroom routine, such as how to organize their notebooks for easy feedback, how to clean up, or how to form a line-up. Once you have criteria that you have set together, then peer and self-assessment are more likely to be purposeful, articulate, and pertinent.

From © 2011 *Making Classroom Assessment Work* (3rd edition) by Anne Davies, p. 62

Then, to provide an opportunity to share across the faculty, consider one or more of the following ideas:

1. Provide time for teachers to explore the ways students are involved in assessment. Consider using a protocol or a

structured conversation to help teachers bring evidence of different aspects of assessment *for* learning: for example, involving students in setting criteria, revisiting rubrics, collecting samples, engaging students in peer and self-assessment, and finding ways to collect and organize evidence, as well as ways to have students share evidence of their learning with others. Consider using one of the 18 conversations from the *Facilitator's Guide to Classroom Assessment K–12* (Davies 2004) or the protocols found on pages 165 and 168.

2. Share implementation ideas—taking time to talk and share craft knowledge is important. Consider using a simple protocol, such as Sticky Issues (see below). Arrange time for teachers to bring back their stories of implementation as they begin to involve students in setting criteria around a project, a process, or a classroom routine: for example, how to organize their notebooks for easy feedback, how to clean up, or how to line up. What worked? What didn't? What do you need to do more? What do you need to do less?

Learning Conversations: Sticky Issues Classroom Assessment Conversation

This conversation is to help participants deepen their understanding and their thinking about classroom assessment issues that currently seem to be sticky issues.

Guidelines:
- Facilitator keeps time and calls time.
- Facilitator reviews or affirms ground rules.
- Facilitator reminds participants of ground rules if needed.
- Remember, this conversation is not about advice; it is about expanding our thinking.
- Unless presenting, do not talk about your school or your situation.

Groups of 4 Plus Facilitator:
Record on an index card a sticky issue you have at this time with regard to classroom assessment. Write a few lines about your dilemma. Then, frame the sticky issue into a question. Review all the sticky issues. Select one person and his/her sticky issue to begin.

1. A presents a sticky issue concerning classroom assessment. (5 minutes) Record the sticky issue on the board/chart so everyone can refer to it. Talk about the dilemma you face. B, C, & D are silent.
2. B, C, & D ask clarifying questions. A answers briefly. (3 minutes)
3. B, C, & D discuss what they have heard about the dilemma. A is silent. A listens and takes notes about what is being said that is helping stretch his/her thinking about the dilemma. Their dialogue focuses on the following:
   - What seems to be the primary issue?
   - What questions does the sticky issue raise for you?
   - What didn't you hear that you wonder about? (8 minutes)
4. A speaks to what was said that helped to stretch her/his thinking. Others are silent as she/he speaks.
5. A, B, C, & D closure. (4 minutes) Start with A sharing how the process helped her with the issue. Then B, C, and D comment.
6. Facilitator calls time and closes.

Break: After a short stretch, invite another participant to present his or her sticky issue.

The Sticky Issues Protocol can be found as a reproducible on page 166 of appendix 2.

Process adapted from Sticky Issues Protocol developed by Southern Maine Partnership and found in Critical Friends Toolbox. www.essentialschools.org

Being a Lead Learner

Incorporate every aspect of involving students in assessment by thoughtfully and deliberately engaging your adult learners in assessment. Make a plan to introduce one aspect each month. Go slowly. Explain to the adult learners with whom you work that you are new to this and enlist their support. Take a risk. Be a learner. Be seen to be a learner. Ask your colleagues to model for you and mentor your development. Begin with co-constructing criteria in relation to a process, a product, or a collection of evidence and then move on to involving them in self-assessment, setting goals, peer assessment, and so on. Consider modeling quality by using specific, descriptive feedback when you write notes to staff acknowledging their daily work. As you work with adult learners, model involving students in goal setting by working to set goals as a staff or as part of the professional growth portfolio process. Watch for your own opportunities to practice and learn as a lead teacher.

> One superintendent leadership team set criteria with the administrative staff from every school in the district and used the criteria to organize meetings and to promote learning about assessment *for* learning. A "note-out-the-door" feedback technique was part of every meeting, which modeled assessment *for* learning by using feedback for continuous improvement.

> In another district, professional development leaders used the self-assessment process with teachers to help them indicate their own learning needs in regard to assessment for learning. A checklist, such as the one on the facing page called *Closing the Achievement Gap*, can facilitate this process.

Closing the Achievement Gap

Self-Assessment Checklist for Learner Involvement	Met	On the Way...	Beginning	Evidence
1. Learners are able to articulate the learning destination and understand what success looks like.				
2. Learners have access to samples that show quality work.				
3. Learners are able to describe what evidence of learning might look like.				
4. Learners set criteria *with* teachers to define quality.				
5. Learners have time to learn.				
6. Learners receive and give themselves specific, descriptive feedback as they learn.				
7. Learners debrief their learning with their peers and others, and get feedback for learning.				
8. Learners use feedback and self-assess to set goals for future learning.				
9. Learners revisit and reset the criteria as they learn more.				
10. Learners collect evidence of their own learning.				
11. Learners present evidence of learning to others and receive feedback. They have opportunities to improve the quality of their evidence of learning. Evaluation is based on evidence collected from multiple sources over time.				
12. Learners are authentically engaged in the learning–assessment process. They are working harder and learning more.				
13. Reports are based on triangulated data (multiple sources).				

An outline of this self-assessment checklist can be found as a reproducible on page 167 of appendix 2.

Planning to Walk the Talk

Consider one way to walk your talk during the coming week. Record your commitment. Consider using a digital camera to collect evidence of your walking the talk.

- Use the Sticky Issues Protocol (described on page 71 and found as a reproducible on page 166) with your leadership colleagues. Notice whether useful ideas emerge. Notice how it feels to participate.

- Pick one part of your job and thoughtfully apply these ideas. For example, with your support staff, set criteria around something that needs clarifying. You might start with questions such as:

    - What is important when answering the telephone?
    - What is important when dealing with complaints?
    - What is important when interacting with students?

Remember to follow brainstorming rules and record the list of ideas.

- Share your self-assessments with staff, and include self-assessment as part of the school planning process, as well as all performance assessments.

Place copies or pictures of your work in your draft portfolio collection.

Using Assessment to Guide Instruction

"Assessment that works in the interests of children will enhance their ability to see and understand their learning for themselves, to judge it for themselves, and to act on their judgments."

Mary Jane Drummond

Assessment *for* learning teaches students, while helping them learn how to assess their way to success. Daily involvement in classroom assessment builds a strong foundation for learning. What does this process look like in a classroom? This chapter presents an example of what assessment and instruction can look like. In this example, students are learning how to conduct a research project. As you read, consider being a witness to students who are engaged in the assessment process, and reflect on the indicators of classroom application. Let's begin.

Talking About the Learning

We are going to be working on a research project over the next few weeks. It is important for you to learn how to gather information and make sense of it for yourself and for your life. Think about the Internet. There is a lot of information available, but for it to be of any use, you have to decide what you want to know, make choices about what information to take seriously and what to ignore, and then decide what it all means for you. That's being a critical thinker—a thoughtful user of information. So, what do you think is important about a research project?

When students are engaged in conversation about any learning activity or task beforehand, the talk clarifies options, highlights possible plans, and encourages sharing information with others.

As students work with teachers to define what learning is and what it looks like, they shift from being passive learners to being actively involved in their own learning. By being engaged, they use and build more neural pathways in their brains. This means they are more likely to be able to access their learning more easily and for a longer period of time—far beyond the end of the unit or test.

When teachers talk about what is to be learned and why it is relevant to students' lives, and invite students to define what it might look like once they've learned it, students begin to understand what needs to be learned and have a chance to prepare to learn. Many learning theorists propose that we interpret the world through our mental models—that is, we see what we expect to see and hear what we expect to hear. Brain research supports this perspective (Pert 1999; Pinker 1997; Restak 2003; Rock 2009). When students are involved from the beginning, they are more ready to learn. When we involve students in shaping their learning, they are more likely to:

- Understand what is expected of them
- Access prior knowledge
- Have some ownership over making it happen
- Be able to give themselves descriptive feedback as they are learning
- Give information that teachers need to adjust their teaching

Knowing what they are learning and what it looks like gives students the information they need to assess *themselves* as they learn—to keep themselves on track. Learning to self-monitor in this way is an essential skill for independent, self-directed, lifelong learners.

Showing Samples and Discussing the Evidence

I am going to give you several examples of research projects. Here is a poster, a video, a booklet, and a timeline. I want you to work in groups to analyze these student projects and think about what is really important in a research project. Especially think about how information is effectively communicated. When you are ready, we will list your ideas and create criteria for our research project. We can record the criteria on a T-chart so you can refer to it as you work.

When teachers give students samples to review and talk with them about what is important in their learning, they help them build mental models of what success looks like. This is particularly important for the students who struggle the most.

When teachers spend time with students, sharing samples as well as connecting what students already know to what they need to know, it increases students' understanding of what they will be learning and of what will be assessed. Being involved in this way helps them use their prior knowledge and learn more about the language of learning and assessment. Students also begin to understand what evidence looks like and to find out what is important—what matters.

Getting on With the Learning

It's time for you to get started on your research projects. We are going to begin with a small one so you can all practice with the support of a group before you do a larger research project independently. This is also a chance for you to find out what you already know about doing a research project and a chance to learn from your group members.

For this first project, I would like you to work in small groups. I want your group to choose something you are interested in learning more about. Choose something where the information will be easy to find, since you will only have a week to do this research project. Perhaps it will be something you already know a lot about, such as a sport, music, or pets. Think of topics that interest you and your classmates. In a week's time, your group will make a presentation to the class. At that time, we will be using the criteria we created to assess your work. Keep it in mind as you are working.

Giving students time to discover what they already know and to learn from each other provides a scaffold for future learning. When conversations about learning take place in the group, learners can check their thinking and performance and develop deeper understanding of their learning. Researchers studying the role of emotions and the brain say that experiences such as these prepare learners to take the risks necessary for learning (Goleman 1996; Le Doux 1996; Pert 1999).

Presenting

> Class, you've had a week to work on your research projects. Tomorrow you'll be presenting your work to your classmates. Please sign up with Terry and Cheryl if you want your presentation recorded on video. It will be your decision whether or not to include the video in your portfolio.
>
> Remember our purpose. This is a chance for you to find out what you already knew about doing a research project, as well as to learn from your group members. As I said before, we are going to use the criteria we agreed on to assess your work. After you do your presentations, I will ask each group to self-assess. I will also be using the criteria we developed to give feedback. Any questions?

Some students know what teachers want without it having to be explained in detail. It seems others simply don't get it. When we make the criteria explicit, share the process of learning with each other, and give descriptive feedback according to the agreed-upon criteria, we give others the opportunity to learn. We begin to make more of the implicit expectations explicit.

Self-Assessment and Goal Setting

> As you think about your work, I want you to review the criteria we set together. Take a few moments and write in your journal the things that you noticed you were able to do well and two things you need to work on next.

When students and teachers self-assess, they confirm, consolidate, and integrate new knowledge. Debriefing after the learning provides an opportunity for collaborative feedback—from student and teacher perspectives. What do we think we learned? What worked? What didn't? What might we do differently next time?

When students self-assess, they gain insights that help them monitor their learning, as well as practice in giving themselves descriptive feedback. When student self-assessments are shared with teachers, teachers gain a better understanding about where students are in relation to where they need to be.

Research Connection:

Self-assessment asks students to make choices about what to focus on next in their learning. When students make choices about their learning, achievement increases; when choice is absent, learning decreases (Deci and Ryan 2002; Harlen and Deakin Crick 2003).

When students self-assess in relation to criteria or samples of student work, they are giving themselves feedback. Because this feedback takes place in the context of explicit criteria that students have helped to set, it is more likely to help students understand what needs to be done differently. Explicit criteria and samples of student work help increase the possibility that when students interact with an audience—peers, parents, teachers, and others—and receive feedback, the next steps in their learning will be more informed.

Please look at the criteria and your self-assessment, and think about what you need to focus on the next time. This will become your goal. Do not take on too many things—one or two goals are about all anyone can handle. Record one or two goals, what your first steps are going to be, and who you are going to partner with for support.

Revisiting Criteria

Now that you have completed the research project, it is time to revisit the criteria we set. I noticed that some groups did things that weren't part of our criteria on our T-chart. Your presentations and projects may have reminded you of other things that make a research project powerful. Does anyone have any ideas about what needs to be added, changed, or taken away?

As students learn and assess, they define and redefine the criteria. Over time, the criteria become increasingly more specific, as students discover how to apply their learning and produce high-quality work. It is important that the criteria allow for the many different ways students may select to represent the results of their research. For example, when carefully constructed, the same criteria can be used effectively for a timeline, a poster, a written project, or a model.

When students work together to set criteria, self-assess, and revise criteria, they come to understand the process of assessment and they practice using the language of assessment. This way, students gain a clear picture of what they need to learn and where they are in relation to where they need to be, making it possible for them to begin to identify next steps in their learning. Setting goals is a powerful way to focus students' learning.

Ongoing Assessment *for* Learning

Class, before you leave today, I'd like you to fill out the card on your desk. Let me know two things you've learned about research projects and one question you have. Thank you.

When we think about what we've done, we may come to understand it in a different way. Pausing in the learning to self-assess gives learners the opportunity to think about their thinking and their learning—a process called *metacognition*. Students who are able to self-assess—that is, to reflect on *how* they learn—are better able to monitor their own learning process (see accompanying figure). These approaches may be particularly important for children who do not have extra support for learning outside the classroom. When students share their thinking with teachers, students learn more and teachers can teach better. Michael Fullan (2001) put it this way: "An event is not an experience until you reflect upon it."

Note Out the Door

Two things I learned:
1. It takes 6 seconds for food to reach the stomach from the mouth.

2. what the esophagus does.

One question I have:
1. what do the 2 intestines do?

Using Assessment in the Service of Learning

Deliberately using the processes of classroom assessment in support of learning helps students come to know the *how* of learning as well as *what* needs to be learned. Involving students in their own assessment leads to greater student ownership and investment in the learning than when the responsibility for assessment (and for learning) rests entirely with the teacher.

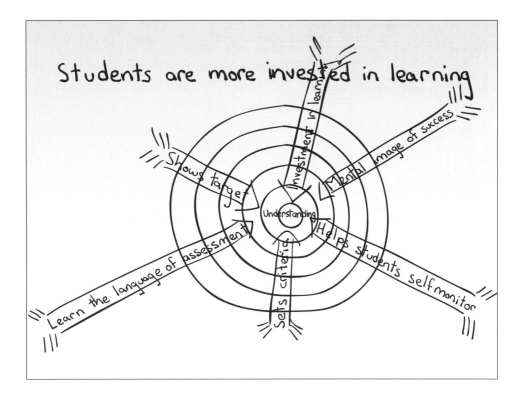

As students become more involved in the assessment process, teachers find themselves working differently. They used to be solely responsible for providing information about the learning. Now there are as many information sources for students as there are models, exemplars, samples, posted criteria, and peers. Many teachers are spending less time grading at the end of the learning and more time helping students during the learning. As teachers find more ways to involve students and increase the amount of descriptive feedback, while decreasing the evaluative feedback, they are discovering for themselves what Black and Wiliam (1998) found in their research—students are learning more.

Being a Leader

Indicators of Classroom Application

This chapter pulls all the elements of involving students in classroom assessment together so you can imagine assessment *in action*. As you visit and observe in classrooms, watch for the following indicators that teachers are using ongoing assessment information to inform teaching and learning.

1. How are teachers checking the learning before deciding what to do next?
2. How are teachers giving specific, descriptive feedback during the learning and having students give themselves and others specific, descriptive feedback?
3. How are teachers focused on collecting evidence of improvement (rather than merely recording what students do not know)?
4. How are teachers involving students, the people most able to improve the learning, in the assessment process?

Supporting Classroom Teachers

Continue to support teachers to build an assessment plan in one subject area by providing time to read chapter 7 in *Making Classroom Assessment Work* and completing the tasks at the end of the chapter. These are shown on the facing page.

Guiding Our Own Learning

Think about a time when students in your classroom were most engaged in learning. Reflect on the following questions:

- What was happening? What were they doing?
- Where were you? What were you doing?
- Did students know the learning destination?
- Did they know what was expected of them in terms of doing the learning?
- Did they know what kind of evidence they would need to produce?
- Were they able to self-monitor in relation to models, criteria, and/or samples?

Record your thoughts.

Guiding the Learning of Students

Ask students to build a list of criteria in response to the question, What do good teachers do that supports your learning? Listen and reflect on their responses in terms of your own teaching.

From © 2011 *Making Classroom Assessment Work* (3rd edition) by Anne Davies, p. 72

If the ideas in this chapter are new to you and the teachers with whom you work, lead learners will need to help classroom teachers to take the first steps. Devote time to collaboratively learn more about assessment *for* learning before expecting implementation in the classrooms, school, or district/division.

Seek resources. Teachers appreciate learning about classroom-tested ideas. Recommend that teachers start with one technique, such as involving students in setting criteria, and take the time needed to transform it from idea to habit.

Provide opportunities. Teachers need chances to connect with colleagues, in order to share and refine techniques that worked and didn't work. Encourage conversations about what teachers can *stop* doing—maybe some of that evaluative marking and grading—in order to have time to involve students in the assessment process.

Develop craft knowledge. Provide time during department, grade-level, learning team, and faculty meetings for colleagues to share ideas and experiences with regards to involving students in assessment. This provides time for the deliberate accumulation of craft knowledge. Incorporate a conversation protocol for analyzing teaching dilemmas so teachers can have the assistance of their colleagues to figure out their own teaching challenges. The Sticky Issues Protocol (described on page 71 and found as a reproducible on page 166 of appendix 2) provides a vehicle to share craft knowledge.

Involve learners. It may be difficult for beginners to appreciate the benefits of having learners participate in the assessment process. The Clapping Activity on page 85 provides a great illustration of how learner involvement can make a difference. Try this activity with your colleagues, and encourage them to use it with students. One principal used this with his principal and district leadership colleagues.

Analyze student work. Incorporate a conversation protocol for analyzing student work so teachers can become more experienced at understanding quality and more able to give specific, descriptive feedback. This also helps to build a common language of assessment among teachers, which can become a part of every classroom over time. Consider inviting principals to bring evidence of quality teaching and use a protocol to look deeply at the collection of evidence.

The Clapping Activity

Purpose: To help students understand why they need to be involved in the classroom assessment process.

Variation: If you have a DJ and music available, consider dancing rather than clapping.

Directions

1. Invite eight volunteers to sit in groups of four facing the audience. They should also be able to view each other easily.
2. Be ready to record. Have on hand chart paper or a whiteboard to record criteria.
3. Explain to the audience that they are about to see a demonstration that will show the history of involving students in classroom assessment. Note that each example occurs over time so it is not helpful to compare one to the other as if they are all happening at the same point in time. Explain that the job of the audience is to listen and become involved only when asked. Then, name one group of four "Judges" and the other group "Participants."
4. Number the participants in each group from one to four.
5. Ask Participant #1 to clap.
6. When #1 finishes, say, "Thank you." (If participant looks surprised, let it be. I usually quietly check back with this person later to make sure she or he is still okay. In my experience the person is fine and later ends up debriefing and talking about how it feels to not know what to do or how to do it.)
7. Ask the judges to award 1, 2, 3, or 4 points, with 4 being the highest. Discourage discussion. Ask the judges to not report out to others.
8. Ask #2 to clap. When #2 is finished say, "Thank you," and send #2 from the room for a few minutes. While #2 is out of the room, ask the judges to score the clapping 1 to 4. Invite the judges to discuss the scoring quietly amongst them. Ask for individual scores, as well as one thing the person did well and one thing they need to work on to get better at clapping. Add all the scores together. Invite #2 back into the room and announce the combined score as well as something to work on.
9. Turn to #3 and hesitate. Ask participant #3 to wait and then turn and ask the judges to list all the characteristics of a really good clap. Record their responses on chart paper. Encourage them to think of everything.
10. Turn to #3 again and say, "Number 3, knowing all this, could you clap for us please?" When #3 finishes, say, "Thank you."
11. Ask the judges, "Given the criteria and the performance, what score would you give, and why?" Give them time to discuss it prior to reporting out.
12. When the judges have reported, turn to #4 (who is very, very nervous by now), and ask #4 to tell about a situation in which he or she has needed to clap, such as at a sports or music event. Ask clarifying questions.
13. Draw participant #4's attention to the criteria set for #3 and ask if there is any criterion that needs to be changed.
14. Then, ask the judges if there is any criterion that needs to be changed—added or deleted.
15. Once you have agreement from the judges, invite #4 to imagine an amazing performance and to clap.
16. Ask #4 to self-assess the clapping.
17. Then, ask the judges to score the clapping and provide specific feedback in relation to the criteria.
18. This is the end of the activity. It is time to reflect on what happened. Ask the participants and judges to reflect on their experience and make some connections. While they are thinking, ask the audience to talk about their connections.
19. After 3–4 minutes, debrief in turn with contestants, judges, and audience. Listen for ideas such as:
    - It is important that the standards or outcomes be clearly defined.
    - Unlike competitions such as the Olympics where only some can win, K–12 education needs to ensure all students learn.
    - More learning motivation occurs when students are involved in assessment.
    - Clear standards and student involvement makes evaluation (judging) easier and fairer.
    - The more assessment information available to the participant/learner, the more likely they are to use it and learn from it and succeed.

Adapted from *A Tool Kit for Professional Developers: Alternative Assessment* by Laboratory Network Program.

Being a Lead Learner

Walk the talk by modeling your own learning in terms of assessment *for* learning. Be seen to be taking the same kinds of risks you are asking teachers to take with their learners and with you. Some examples:

- Keep a portfolio of your growth as a professional. Share it during its development.
- Be explicit about the school or district's learning destination and the evidence (both qualitative and quantitative) that will be required.
- Collect, select, and reflect on the evidence gathered in relation to school or district goals.
- Present the evidence of learning (personal, school, and/or district) to a panel of your peers, as well as to the larger community.

Do what you are asking others to do. *Be* a lead learner. Take risks, make mistakes, and learn publicly with good cheer. Go ahead—be brave. Debrief the experience. Learn from it. Go first for the greater good. After all, modeling the capacity to be human and graceful under pressure is very powerful teaching.

Planning to Walk the Talk

Gather a group of your leadership colleagues together. Do the Clapping Activity with them. Debrief it. Make notes about what you noticed. Then, repeat it with your teaching colleagues, a group of students, and a group of parents. What was similar? What was different? Consider other ways you can help people see the power of student involvement in the classroom assessment process. Place your notes in your draft portfolio collection.

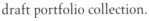

Collecting, Organizing, and Presenting Evidence

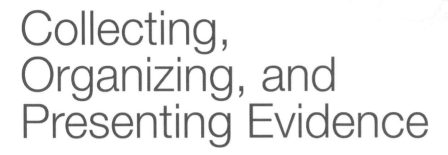

" *The student knows more than the teacher about what and how he has learned—even if he knows less about what was taught.* **"**

Peter Elbow

Collecting, organizing, and presenting evidence of learning used to be the teacher's responsibility alone. Yet if students are to be involved in assessment *in support of* their learning, then they must also be involved in this crucial aspect. Part of learning is recognizing when you've succeeded. You know you've succeeded when you see the evidence. Learners need to collect and organize their evidence, in relation to the learning destination, so they know that they are learning. They need to present their evidence so that others will also know they are learning. That's what it means to be accountable.

Further, in order to have all the evidence needed for balanced and fair assessment, it isn't enough that teachers review work (complete or incomplete) once, record the grade or score, and then file or send the work home. Evidence of learning can potentially be anything students create, do, or articulate. The question of what constitutes the "best" collection of evidence can't be determined in advance. Instead, students need to be involved in gathering and creating comprehensive collections of evidence—that is, products, self-assessments, and recorded observations. The student's collection of evidence becomes a visual history of her or his learning over time. When it is time to evaluate, students can present their best collection of evidence of learning in relation to the learning destination along with reasons why the evidence is good evidence. Then, teachers can review the evidence students have collected and organized, as well as the evidence they have collected, prior to making a professional judgment regarding how much and how well students have learned in relation to what they needed to learn.

Making the Process Work

There are seven parts to ensuring that collecting and organizing evidence supports student learning:

1. State purpose.
2. Identify audience.
3. Keep it simple.
4. Collect.
5. Select and present.
6. Take the time.
7. Invite feedback.

State purpose. Be clear about the three purposes for collecting evidence of learning. The first purpose is to provide proof of learning in relation to the learning destination. This means more than collecting that which is easy to collect, such as tests, quizzes, and common assessment task results. Learning destinations include both process and content. Evidence of learning in relation to the standards or outcomes for the course or subject area needs to be collected from multiple sources over time and will include products, observations of process, and conversations with students (recorded in some way—in writing, self-assessments, notes, observations, audio, or video). The second purpose is to ensure that evidence of learning is present so the teacher can make informed professional judgments during and at the end of the learning term. The third purpose is to ensure the evidence of learning is present to provide documentation that "backs up" the report card grades and provides a "window" into the learning for others.

Identify audience. When the audience is identified, both the kind of evidence of learning as well as the form becomes clear. Because learning destinations are clearly expressed, teachers, students, parents, and others have access to the information they need when they need it. For example, during the term, teachers and students need access to the ongoing evidence of learning so as to guide next steps in learning and teaching. Parents may also want to have access. At the end of the term, the full collection is examined and key pieces selected to show the learning that has occurred over time, as well as to show whether or not the student has reached the expected quality and success levels. Students and teachers continue to be a key audience; however, parents and others become the more formally involved as part of the reporting process.

Keep it simple. What does the teacher collect? What do students collect? This is a teacher-by-teacher decision and depends on professional preferences. Many teachers choose to have students collecting and managing, with their guidance and supervision, the qualitative evidence of learning. After all, students need to be accountable for their learning—which benefits both themselves and their teachers. When students are responsible for assembling the evidence, they have more opportunities to figure out whether they are on track with their learning. It is the teacher's job to show them how to do it well. Teachers decide the balance of teacher work and student involvement that is comfortable—there is no right or wrong way. The balance between teacher-collected evidence and student-collected evidence will vary from year to year and class to class. Teachers need to remember that *the person who is working the hardest is learning the most.* Or, as Pat Wolfe writes, "Remember that the person doing the work is growing the dendrites" (p. 187).

Research Connection:

> Research shows that when students are involved in the assessment process—by co-constructing the criteria by which they are assessed, self-assessing in relation to the criteria, giving themselves information to guide (or "feed-forward") their learning, collecting and presenting evidence of their learning, and reflecting on their strengths and needs—they learn more, achieve at higher levels, and are more motivated. They are also better able to set informed, appropriate learning goals to further improve their learning (Black and Wiliam 1998; Crooks 1988; Davies 2004; Stiggins 2007).

Collect. Collecting evidence of learning from multiple sources over time ensures that the evidence of learning is more likely to be both reliable and valid. It is more reliable because it is repeatable—it is obvious that students have been able to do, show, and articulate that which is important to learn not just once on a high-stakes assessment, but more than once during the learning time. The evidence of learning is more likely to be valid if the classroom instructional plan has been made in relation to all of the learning outcomes or standards, not just those that can be easily evaluated using tests, projects, or other products. The qualitative evidence collected can be designed to show evidence of the full range of student learning represented by the standards or outcomes.

Select and present. When students select from their collections of evidence, they are more likely to recognize progress for themselves. Students can use their collections to show teachers and parents what they know and what they need to learn. This process helps students better understand their own learning and their progress. Again, a range of evidence collected over time and across different tasks increases the validity and reliability of the assessment and evaluation for everyone. When they present this collection to others, it forms a rich resource for reporting. The collection of evidence of learning enlarges the view of what has been learned and provides a window into the student's thinking that gives a multidimensional view of the student as a learner. The more extensive the collection of evidence, the better view it gives of the student's abilities.

Take the time. It is important that teachers take the time to have students do a good job of collecting the evidence of learning. It is also important that teachers collect what is needed to be accountable should parents or others require the backup documentation—evidence—for a particular comment or report card grade. Taking time to support students as they assume a larger role in collecting their own assessment evidence is worthwhile, because students have an opportunity to become more responsible and involved in their own learning and, as a result, learn more.

Invite feedback. Receiving feedback from people whose opinion you value can increase one's motivation to learn. Students' collections of evidence help improve the quality and specificity of communications, including feedback, between teachers, students, and parents. Showing collections of evidence to parents helps to demystify the learning process and provides the information they need to be partners in assessment. It is important to do because students know their audience (their parents, family members, and teachers) and what evidence will help them understand and appreciate the learning.

In closing, gathering and preparing collections of evidence for an audience (e.g., teachers and parents) helps students to learn and practice organizational skills, to take pride in their work, and to discover their own learning styles. Developing skills to collect evidence and present themselves and their learning to others prepares students for life. In a growing number of jurisdictions, student report cards contain a section that reports on student work habits or study skills. Many teachers are involving students in collecting evidence of their own habits of mind—given the discipline being studied.

"*Life is complex. Each one of us must make his own path through life. There are no self-help manuals, no formulas, no easy answers. The right road for one is the wrong road for another. . . . The journey of life is not paved in blacktop; it is not brightly lit, and it has no road signs. It is a rocky path through the wilderness.*"

M. Scott Peck

Being a Leader

Indicators of Classroom Application

As you observe in classrooms, notice:

- How are students using their collections to show teachers and parents what they know and what they need to learn?
- How are students' collections of evidence showing they are working towards quality?
- In what ways are communications focused on learning between teachers, students, and parents addressing what students need to do to improve?
- How are collections of evidence helping students learn and practice organizational skills, take pride in their work, and discover their own preferences and learning styles?
- What kinds of skills are students developing as they present themselves and their learning to others?
- How is the task of providing evidence—proof of learning— shared with students? How is the picture of each student's learning more complete—more valid and reliable—as a result?
- In what ways are conversations regarding evaluation and reporting explored and discussed more fully because the evidence of learning, beyond grades or marks, is present?

Supporting Classroom Teachers

After teachers have an opportunity to read chapter 8 in *Making Classroom Assessment Work* and complete the end-of-chapter tasks, consider your own work. How could you as a leader model the assessment practices described in chapter 8 (and shown on the facing page)? Lead learners support classroom teachers not only by providing time and resources, but also by modeling quality classroom assessment practices in their own work. For example:

In one school, the schoolwide goal was to improve scores on the state assessment in the area of constructed responses in mathematics. The classroom portfolios had three pockets for student work in relation to classroom learning goals, and a fourth pocket was designated for constructed responses in mathematics.

In another district, school leadership teams were asked to collect evidence of their implementation of assessment *for* learning and to bring evidence of their learning to districtwide gatherings to share with others. Some school teams chose to compile a professional portfolio showing evidence of growth over time.

Guiding Our Own Learning

Ask your colleagues how their students are involved in organizing and collecting evidence of their learning. Listen for ideas that might help you, as well as ways to make it easier to involve students. Record the ideas.

Think about the evidence your students need to produce and what you want the audience to learn about as they view the evidence collection. Record your thoughts. Consider them as you design the ways your students will collect, reflect, and share their learning with others. Once your plan is complete, put it into action.

Guiding the Learning of Students

Continue to involve students in assessing for success:

- Ask them to collect evidence of learning in relation to one unit of study. Remind them that different students may have different kinds of proof, depending on how they choose to show what they've been learning.
- Periodically ask them to find proof of meeting one standard or learning outcome, and record why they feel their evidence is proof.
- Encourage them to use the language of the criteria you set together to guide their self-assessment.

From © 2011 *Making Classroom Assessment Work* (3rd edition) by Anne Davies, p. 84

Here are some ideas to consider:

1. *Provide time.* Make sure teachers have scheduled time to share the ways they are involving students in organizing and collecting evidence of their learning. Invite them to listen for ideas that might assist them in their classes.

2. *Plan collections of evidence.* Encourage classroom teachers to think about the evidence their students need to produce and what they want the audience to witness and learn as they view the students' collections of evidence. Ask teachers to bring their ideas, as well as actual samples of students' collections of evidence, sample observation sheets, and stories of how they involve students in building a language of assessment to improve feedback to self and others. The "Evidence of Learning Interview" (Davies 2004) is a useful tool to help uncover colleagues' practices and share the ideas beyond just one classroom. (See the Interview Questions on the opposite page.)

3. *Collect and share practical ideas.* Gather resources concerning portfolio collections together, and bring them to a faculty meeting. Have people do a quick scan to see one or two ideas of interest prior to sharing across table groups. Then, focus conversation among teachers across a grade level or within a department, so that together they identify strategies for organizing their record-keeping, as well as their students' collections of work samples. (A Sample Selection Protocol is shown on page 97.)

Interview Questions

Question	Response
What's the best way you have of collecting or keeping track of evidence?	
What part of collecting or keeping evidence do you do, and what part do the students do?	
How do you make sure your findings are reliable and valid?	
What's one part of your process you want to improve?	
What is one thing you are spending too much time on? Too little time on?	
What new ideas are you planning to try out?	

From © 2004 *Facilitator's Guide to Classroom Assessment K–12* by Anne Davies (H1 Evidence of Learning)

Being a Lead Learner

Finding ways to model and walk the talk can be difficult because, as leaders, we tend to dismiss as unimportant the small things we might do. Some of these are:

- Keeping our own growth portfolio
- Making and sharing notes from observations in classrooms, focused on the use of assessment *for* learning strategies
- Asking teachers to self-assess as part of the professional growth process
- Writing notes to give teachers and other staff specific, descriptive feedback so they can generate rich evidence
- Providing rich evidence in relation to the school or district plan

We must always be looking for opportunities to model and walk the talk. When we fail to model assessment *for* learning, those who are watching us may use our lack of action as a reason not to change.

For example, if we have worked with our adult learners and defined together what quality assessment looks and sounds like, we can ask them to let us know when our actions fail to model quality classroom assessment practices. If you have worked with your adult learners and defined together what quality assessment looks and sounds like, you can ask them to let you know when you have failed to model quality classroom assessment practices, as well as provide specific ideas as to what you might do differently. Be prepared to receive advice by using active listening skills *(listen, restate, and clarify)* and appreciation, even when the feedback is upsetting or seems unwarranted. If needed, ask for time to reflect before responding. Thank the brave person who spoke up, and discuss your questions with him or her until resolution is reached. Publicly acknowledge your mistakes and your intention to rectify and to avoid the same error in future. Being a leader is a challenging and rich opportunity for learning.

Sample Selection Protocol

Purpose of the Protocol: To collect a range of samples that represents work from a grade level.

Prior to the Conversation: The facilitator identifies a focus question (i.e., Would you agree that this work represents the range of work—developing, on the way, exceeding—for this grade level?).

(2 minutes)
Getting Started: Select a facilitator and a timekeeper. Review the purpose of the protocol and ground rules for this process. Be sure everyone has brought samples created by students in response to the same task. Note: student and teacher names should be removed.

This protocol can be found as a reproducible on page 168 of appendix 2.

(5 minutes)
Context: The facilitator offers any background information and the purpose for the assessment. The focus question is written on chart paper or board for all to see.

(5 minutes)
Review: The group members review the student work in regard to the focus question. (If student work is lengthy, the work and the focus question may be given ahead of time.)

(12 minutes)
Group Discussion: Using the focus question as their guide, group members generate their insights and observations by what they see in the work. The facilitator moderates the discussion.

(5 minutes)
The group selects and organizes two or three samples as exemplars of each level (e.g. developing, on the way, exceeding) to show the range of work found at the grade level in response to the task.

(5 minutes)
Reflection on the Conversation: The group members discuss how they experienced this protocol conversation and what they learned.

Adapted with permission from *Protocols for Professional Learning Conversations* by Catherine Glaude (2011).

Think about your role. What are you aiming to achieve as you work toward assessment *for* learning? Record it. Then, list all the evidence you have of your effectiveness in your role.

Take time to interview two or three colleagues in different roles in your workplace. Ask them to give you one example of a time when you were effective and one example of a time when you could have been more effective. Take notes. Add the notes to your evidence collection in your draft portfolio.

Periodically, as you sort your files and desktop (digital and physical), place anything that is evidence of your effectiveness into a file or a box. Then, when you have a need to show proof, perhaps as part of the evaluation process, you can select, reflect, and organize the evidence with a particular purpose and audience in mind. This process will help you understand the complexity and importance of the process of collecting both qualitative and quantitative evidence.

Communicating About Learning

Contents

"We can tell a little more of the truth. In doing so, it turns out that we can avoid pretending that a student's whole performance or intelligence can be summed up in one number."

Peter Elbow

In the past, informal communications—such as conversations in the parking lot, by the boot racks, in the local market, or on the lanai, as well as notes or a telephone call to the parents—helped build partnerships between home and school. Casual communications such as these kept students, their families, and teachers in step with each other.

As family life grows busier and more complex, social media takes a greater role, and the information glut overwhelms even the most organized of us. We may feel we have less time to become informed. Yet many parents want to know more about their child's education. Adding to the challenge is the increasing diversity and changing values of our communities. Sometimes we might wonder if there is a common meeting place—there is. Families, schools, and teachers come together in caring about the student. We all want the best for each one of them, even though we may express it in different ways.

Successful Communications

One solution to the challenge of finding ways to communicate is through involving students. Celebrating our accomplishments by sharing our work with others is part of the learning process. The audience can be made up of classmates, other classes, parents and guardians, or community members. They may be present to one another directly or via email or the Internet. When the learning is captured in print or in digital form, it becomes concrete evidence that can be used later, for students' conferences and in reports to others. And as students come to understand what they have learned, what they need to learn, and what kind of support may be available to them, they prepare for more learning. As they receive feedback and recognition from themselves and from others that guide and support their learning, they identify specific next steps. The process of preparing and presenting gives students an opportunity to construct their understanding and to help others make meaning of their learning. This provides supported practice in self-monitoring—where am I going, where am I now, what do my next steps need to be—an essential skill for self-directed, independent, lifelong learners.

When parents and others watch demonstrations of learning or attend student–parent conferences, it increases their appreciation of their son or daughter as a learner, his or her level of skill development, the breadth of the classroom and school curriculum, and the efforts needed on everyone's behalf to make learning possible. When the audience is invited to respond, they acknowledge and support the learning, while giving students valuable feedback.

There are four parts to successful communication about learning:

1. Learners collect and prepare evidence of learning.
2. Learners show or demonstrate their learning.
3. Audience reviews and responds.
4. Feedback supports ongoing learning.

Examples of successful communications include e-newsletters, email, texting, social networking sites, class websites, self-assessments shared with an audience, work samples including a viewing guide, demonstrations with guided questions and feedback such as reading a book, a science experiment, playing a musical instrument, online student–parent conferences, and before- and after-work samples.

Gregory et al. (2011) have included ten ways for students to show evidence of their learning to others during the term and also describe how to involve students in student-parent-teacher conferences. (For more ideas, see *Conferencing and Reporting* by Gregory, Cameron, and Davies.)

Refine Through Feedback

Whenever teachers invite students to communicate about their learning to others, it is important to follow up in order to find out whether it was successful for the students and for the audience. Even with the best of intentions, mistakes are made. Knowing what is working and what is not provides the information needed to help everyone continue to improve.

Encourage teachers to ask students and parents what worked and what did not. Asking for one or two compliments and one piece of advice can be enough (see accompanying figure). Consider keeping surveys anonymous so students and parents will feel more comfortable expressing their thoughts. Let students and parents know what was said by posting a summary of the comments on the class website, or ask students to include it in the next class newsletter home.

Math Night Survey

Dear Students and Parents:

Feedback is essential for learning - we need to know what worked (do more of) and what did not (do less of). Please help us learn to do a better job by responding to this survey. You do not need to sign it, but please send the completed survey back to the school secretary, so it can be put in the collection box in the office.

Thank you.

What are two compliments you have about Math Night?

We could see the growth in our son's work and confidence. We were pleased to see the variety of his math work. I especially liked that he felt in control. He was proud to show his achievements. I also liked his "agenda". He had a specific order to his work. He was well prepared.

Is there anything you'd like to see or do next time?

It is important for our son to show his learning, but we also want to know what you think. Will you be a part of our report card conference next month? Last year the teacher had lots of conferences at one time, and we didn't get a chance to find out what she thought. After our conference this year, can we sign up if we need to talk to you?

Adapted from Politano and Davies, *Multi-Age and More*, p. 107

Finding Your Own Way

When teachers involve students in communicating about their learning, they are inviting thoughtful conversations about learning. There is no one right or best way to do this. In fact, social networking media and mobile technology, such as smartphones, have recently been giving us new ways to interact with others. Teachers need to select the method or combination of methods that work for them, their students, and their families in the school community.

Being a Leader

Successful communication to parents and community members is based on a simple truth—when time is limited, people listen first to those they care about. When it comes to school, parents are most interested in their child's opinions. Of course, parents still value the teacher's assessment and their child's report card, but many are chiefly influenced by their student's beliefs and attitudes about their classroom and the school. When school and district leaders encourage teachers to have students involved in sharing evidence of their learning, we are taking a risk, but we also know that the potential for focusing the conversation on learning is worth it.

As leaders, we need to consider the following questions:

- Do teachers have a communication plan that goes beyond communicating using midterm and end-of-term reports?
- How are students collecting and preparing evidence of learning?
- How are students learning the language of assessment? Can they talk about their learning using specific, descriptive language that relates to the standards or learning outcomes?
- How are students showing or demonstrating their learning to others (inside and outside of school)?
- How are parents and other audiences invited to respond to students with feedback that supports ongoing learning?
- How are faculty members transforming every communication "event" into one that reminds parents and community members of the learning that is going on and invites the audience to give students specific, descriptive feedback?

As you reflect on effective communication opportunities, consider the many different ways community members enter the school or witness learning outside of the school—such as dramatic performances, sporting events, French cafés, Spanish siestas, journalism class publications, or fine arts nights. Are students acting as masters of ceremonies for school events, explaining the learning that has gone on before the public presentation? Are there feedback forms for audience members that explain the learning and ask for their reflections? Do students receive specific feedback? Do faculty members review the feedback and collect pieces as evidence of school goals? (See figure above.)

Supporting Classroom Teachers

Consider inviting teachers to spend some time reflecting on their current communication efforts with a view to streamlining and simplifying them so students can be more engaged and responsible. The tasks at the end of chapter 9 in *Making Classroom Assessment Work* provide a helpful framework for this work. These are shown on the following page.

Guiding Our Own Learning

Record your ideas about your current communication practices. Reflect on the following:

- How do you currently communicate with others about student learning?
- How are students involved?
- How could you increase student involvement?
- What kind of balance is best for the students with whom you work?
- Do your students need to be doing more? How could you simplify the process so they can do more?

With a group of colleagues, share ideas about what works. Gather samples. Talk through simple ways to increase student involvement. Recreate your communication plan.

Guiding the Learning of Students

Begin increasing the involvement of students in communicating their learning journey—their evidence of learning—to others. Consider:

1. Dividing up bulletin board space so students each have a personal display area—when students display their own work, they attach a note that explains why they selected the work sample and what they want the audience to notice about their work.
2. Having students find proof of their learning to share with others, such as:
   - Most improved piece of work
   - Piece of work most in need of editing
   - Piece of work that required the most perseverance
3. Inviting feedback with attached notes, such as: "As you look at my work, please notice. . ."
4. Initiating a simple four-pocket portfolio that highlights the evidence students have created in relation to the course or a subject area's learning destination.

From © 2011 *Making Classroom Assessment Work* (3rd edition) by Anne Davies, p. 92

Some of the challenges of diversity among families become less problematic when students are involved in crafting the communication, because they will tend to adjust or modify it as needed. For example, students will address the communication to the right person or translate it into the home language.

Ask teachers to share ideas about what works with a group of colleagues. Gather samples and display them so that others might adapt the ideas for their practice. Discuss simple but effective ways to increase student involvement. Consider using a focused conversation, as shown in the figure on page 108, to encourage more ideas of simple ways to achieve great results. There are also others to be found in the *Facilitator's Guide to Classroom Assessment K–12* (Davies 2004).

Another way leaders can support classroom teachers is by making it possible for them to involve students in communicating evidence of learning and have it count as part of the classroom, school, or district communication plan. By showing evidence of their learning to parents, students help them understand what education looks like these days. Some of the ways teachers are involving students include:

- Digital opportunities for classroom use, such as Twitter, Facebook, text messaging, and a classroom blog or a class website
- Weekly folders of student work accompanied by a parent feedback form
- Before-and-after folders or online portfolios containing samples of student work that show growth over time
- Evidence of working toward or achieving a goal set by the student
- Asking students to find an audience for an at-home performance using a musical instrument, a math game, or a recipe from cooking class

Schools become a more valued part of the community when families participate in school events. The best way to ensure that parents and community members take part is by having students themselves extend the invitation. There are many ways that teachers can work with students to involve family members in the life of the school and to use these occasions for sharing evidence of their learning. Here are some examples:

- Math nights or family nights
- Student-led conferences
- Displays of student work
- Senior exhibitions
- Online student portfolios and demonstrations
- Goal-setting conferences

It is important that teachers work together to plan and debrief the experiences so they become more refined and easier over time. Not everyone needs to do everything. Different teachers will have different ideas and methods. Leaders can encourage diversity. Discourage parents from assuming that all teachers must communicate in all ways. Communicating can become a burden and, in the end, shift the emphasis away from student learning.

School-based leaders might want to organize some additional school-wide events with students, such as student focus groups or lunchtime input sessions. Take time to ensure your initiatives complement the work already being done by teachers and students.

An elementary school collected samples of reading, writing, and problem-solving across the school. The samples were organized into age levels—5- to 7-year-olds, 8- to 10-year-olds, and 11- to 13-year-olds. Then, each collection of work was displayed in the front entrance, with two paper cut-out children (matching in size to the age group), named Norm and Norma Reference. When parents came for open house or for any other event, this display was there for them to reference.

A school collected samples of reading and writing in a binder and made it available to parents so they could get a picture of development over time.

Another school began an online collection of digital reading "performances" at different ages so parents could see what reading aloud looked and sounded like. These digital clips were available on an intranet accessible to the school community only.

A school took advantage of Voter Days held in the school and had students welcome community members who came to vote during school hours. They offered guided tours of classrooms in action and showed student work.

A school invited students to be representatives at trustee/parent advisory council meetings.

Being a Lead Learner

When they have experienced the process for themselves, teachers will better understand what students need in order to collect, organize, select, and reflect upon their own learning evidence prior to presenting it to others. Consider making this part of the teacher supervision and professional growth process. As a lead learner, consider sharing your own learning evidence with your teaching colleagues. This can help you improve in your role as supervisor. Here are some examples:

- Look for opportunities for receiving feedback from others.
- Ask for 360-degree feedback from all those with whom you work and interact.
- Ask parents and community members for advice and suggestions on how to best communicate with them.
- Invite parents (or students, staff members, or classroom teachers) to be part of a focus group.

Involving Students in Communicating Their Learning

Learning Goal

This conversation will help participants consider reasons and ways to involve students in communicating their learning.

Materials

Print copies of Record Sheet for each person.

Print a Taking Action worksheet for everyone.

A copy of *Conferencing and Reporting* (2nd edition) by Gregory, Cameron, and Davies (2011) for each

Getting Started

To introduce this conversation, summarize pages 13–15 in the text, *Conferencing and Reporting*.

Form groups of five. Distribute the Record Sheet and suggest participants use it to keep track of their thinking during the conversation.

Let participants know they will be participating in a simple jigsaw. They will read the text by assignment then share what they have read.

Person #1 Work Samples p. 18 and Criteria With Evidence pp. 29–30.

Person #2 Portfolio Afternoon pp. 19–22 and Home Performance p. 33.

Person #3 Goal Envelopes pp. 23–25 (top) and Mind Maps pp. 31–32.

Person #4 Subject Stations pp. 25–26 and School Performances p. 34.

Person #5 Picture This pp. 27–28 and Personal Newsletter p. 35.

Ask participants to read, looking for ways to involve students in communicating their learning during the term and also to make connections to successful ideas.

After the reading, invite people to discuss the ideas, questions, and their own connections in their group.

Debriefing the Learning

After participants have finished reporting on the ideas and their personal connections within their small groups, form one large group.

Invite people to share some of the ideas, questions, and connections that arose in the small groups.

Taking Action

Distribute the Taking Action worksheets.

Ask participants to record one communication idea that they are considering trying. Suggest they record their plans on their Record Sheet and tell someone else about their plans. Decide when you will meet again to share your findings with the group.

Extending the Learning

Ask participants to return at a later date to discuss what was tried, what worked, and what didn't. Invite the group to talk about how they adapted the ideas to work with their particular students.

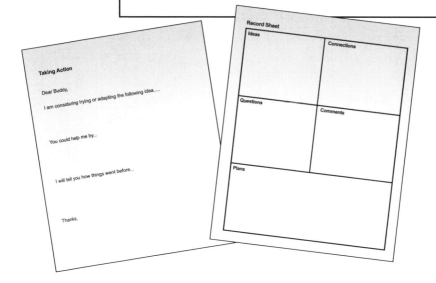

Taking Action

Dear Buddy,

I am considering trying or adapting the following idea.....

You could help me by...

I will tell you how things went before...

Thanks,

Record Sheet

Ideas	Connections
Questions	Comments
Plans	

As you widen your feedback loop, be sure to point out to colleagues the results of your interactions. Communicate clearly how your actions have been influenced by what you've learned from them. Help them see the best ways to teach you and each other.

Lead learners communicate by:

- Publishing school and district learning results
- Organizing displays in the mall/community
- Organizing school and district community events
- Hosting forums to discuss issues of concern
- Creating and sending out newsletters or placing advertisements
- Using digital blogs and online networking

Planning to Walk the Talk

Communication strategies like the following can simplify your role as leader:

1. Make a chart, and list all the people and groups of people with whom you must communicate.
2. Record all the means and methods (big and small) that you currently use to communicate with them.
3. Meet with three or more colleagues in similar roles from different schools and districts. Ask about their audiences as well as their methods. Add potential ideas to your list.
4. Consider reducing your workload by:
    - Collaborating with another person in a similar role from a different jurisdiction and sharing the work
    - Developing materials that could be used more than once over a two- or three-year cycle
    - Looking for overlaps (Do you really need to be carrying the responsibility for all the people and groups on your list, or could some of them be better cared for by others?)

Some jurisdictions prepare multiple years' worth of school newsletter "blurbs" about classroom assessment so parents can be informed over time and the message is expressed in similar ways from school to school.

As you find ways to manage your communications more effectively, you will find ways to help other people—including classroom teachers and students—manage theirs. In today's world of global communication, there are endless ways for schools and families to stay connected in support of their learners. Place your ideas into your draft portfolio collection.

Evaluating and Reporting

"When we give grades or comments that try for objectivity or impersonality or general validity, we are very likely—not to put too fine a point on it—to be telling lies."

Peter Elbow

Evaluation and reporting occur at the point in the classroom assessment cycle when the learning pauses, and the evidence is organized and evaluated by comparing it to what students needed to learn. Then, the results of the evaluation are shared, usually in a conference and/or in a report card. The foundation for evaluating and reporting is put in place when the teacher develops the descriptions of learning (chapter 3), describes what success looks like for students (chapter 4), and thinks through the evidence that will be needed (chapter 5). When it is time to evaluate, teachers revisit the descriptions of learning, review the evidence students have organized, as well as evidence teachers have collected, and then use their professional judgment to make their evaluation. They review their judgment and evidence with students and their parents, and report using the required format. Evaluating and reporting are the last steps in an assessment process that begins much earlier.

Working Together

Evaluating and reporting requires professional judgment in response to the following four issues:

1. What does the student know, what is she or he able to do, and what can she or he articulate?
2. What areas require further attention or development?
3. In what ways can the student's learning be supported?
4. How is the student progressing in relation to the standards or development for students in a similar age range?

Students, parents, and teachers each have a role in the evaluating and reporting process (see accompanying figure).

Three-Way Conference Goal Sheet

Name: _____ Date: _____

Goals I have chosen to work on this year:

Goal 1: improve on home work in math— fewer than 5 wrong

Goal 2: improve on writing skills — write at least 5 writing pieces

Student Will:	Parent Will:	Teacher Will:
show homework to mom. Slow down in math. Ask for help.	GOAL 1. a. CHECK HOMEWORK b. Quiz on MATH FACTS GOAL 2. a. LOOK OVER WRITING PIECES b. MAKE SUGGESTIONS	Correct the math in a timely fashion. Give assistance. Set clear expectations for written pieces.

Students do the learning and along the way, create the evidence of learning. In preparation for evaluation and reporting, they organize the evidence and summarize their strengths, needs, and plans. They present the evidence to account for their learning and listen to feedback. Then, they set goals for future learning.

Parents participate by listening, watching, asking questions, and making sense of the evidence. They interpret the evidence and the accompanying self-assessments that students present, as well as the commentary the teacher gives. To this, they add their own observations of their son or daughter as a learner.

Teachers, because it is their professional responsibility, are the final arbitrators and evaluators of the work. They assist students to communicate their learning to parents, and they make themselves available to discuss how they have evaluated the student's work, as well as ways that student learning could be better supported.

Professional Judgments

Making an informed professional judgment is a purposeful, systematic, multistep process. It begins when teachers come to understand the standards or outcomes in a subject area and the appropriate quality levels expected for a particular course or grade level. It is further informed when teachers meet with others to come to a common understanding of quality and expectations. Then, once the evidence of learning has been collected from multiple sources over time, it is a process of examining the evidence—both qualitative and quantitative—and making a decision regarding whether and to what degree students know, understand, can apply, and can articulate that which is detailed by the standards or outcomes. Professional judgment becomes more informed with reflection, practice, and ongoing collegial conversations that involve looking at student work from classrooms, using protocols, and examining student data generated from a variety of sources.

The evaluating and reporting process includes: evaluating all the evidence of learning, involving students and parents in reviewing the evidence, summarizing strengths and areas needing improvement, and finalizing the report. This process involves using professional judgment. Teachers' professional lives might be simpler if evaluating and reporting could be tidy and objective, but the process of evaluation is inherently subjective. The more reliable and valid the evidence collected and the longer the period of time over which it is collected, the more confidence everyone can have in the evaluation. Also, when students and their parents are engaged in reviewing the evidence and affirming whether or not the evaluation makes sense, sound professional judgments are more likely. By looking for patterns and trends over time, based on multiple sources (triangulation) of reliable and valid evidence, the teacher can report in a professional manner.

Taking Care. . .

In evaluation, teachers must be especially careful when working with numbers from performance scales and rubrics. Totaling scores from rubrics and averaging them with other kinds of numbers is like adding mangoes, potatoes, apples, and trees. The process does not make mathematical sense.

Evaluating the Evidence

Evaluation is a process of looking at all the evidence, comparing it to the description and samples of quality, and asking: "Did this student learn what was to be learned? How well?" When we evaluate, we determine the worth or value of the evidence—we appraise it with respect to excellence or merit. Simply totaling the marks or grades in our record book means that important evidence may not be considered. To evaluate well, we should look at *all* the evidence—observations, products, and conversations.

Triangulation of evidence is essential because it puts single pieces of evidence into context. As a judge in a court of law must examine all the evidence in light of the legal statutes, teachers must look at all the evidence in light of the description of learning. They must consider the entire range of indicators—the evidence students have collected, the self-assessments they have made, teachers' observations, criteria-based assessments attached to projects or assignments, performance rubrics, rubric scores, and grades from projects and tests. (Review chapter 5 for more information regarding evidence of learning.) We can then use this evidence to determine whether the student has met the widely held expectations for his or her age.

Reporting

Reporting used to be a special event that happened only at set times in a year. Now it is an ongoing process that involves students, parents, and teachers in examining and making sense of a student's learning.

Informal reporting happens every time students speak with their parents about learning, take home a sample of their work and discuss it, or invite parents to a portfolio viewing in school, at home, or online to look at their work or to participate in a student-parent-teacher conference (see figure on facing page).

Formal evaluating and reporting is usually required by legislation or policy and is a process of looking at the evidence, having conversations and conferences about what the evidence means, and keeping a written record of the conversation for the learner's permanent file.

Increasingly, teachers are involving students in the conferencing and reporting process and inviting them and their parents to be part of student-parent-teacher conferences. The purpose of these conferences is to look at the evidence, highlight strengths, discuss areas needing improvement, and set goals during the reporting period.

Mid-Term Informal Report

By:_____

My personal goal for this term was:

_____
_____
_____

Please notice how I:
- have achieved my goal.
- am working on my goal.
- am thinking about starting to work on my goal.

You can know this because:

_____
_____

Parent(s)' Comments:

_____
_____
_____

Parent(s)' Signature(s): _____

Teacher's Signature: _____

Date: _____

Being a Leader

Indicators of Classroom Application

Reporting to parents is a legal obligation, and as a result, there are penalties if it is not done correctly. As a school or district leader, you have an obligation to make sure rules and regulations are followed in order to ensure that educators and students who depend upon you are protected.

As leaders, we need to help teachers figure out which processes of evaluation and reporting will work for them, their students, and their parents, in the given situation. As leaders, we assist teachers to:

- Work within the legal requirements for reporting in their schools and districts
- Develop an assessment plan that summarizes the learning destination and the evidence of learning, and collect samples to illustrate quality
- Develop a description of achievement
- Involve students in the classroom assessment process
- Collect samples of growth over time
- Involve students in collecting and organizing the evidence
- Spend time examining the evidence and doing their own evaluation
- Check with students to ensure the teacher's evaluation of their work made sense
- Ask parents to review the evidence and invite them to also do a "report" from their perspective
- Meet with each student and her or his parents to discuss strengths, areas needing improvement, and goals
- Inform parents clearly as to whether or not their child's learning was in the "safety zone" or whether intervention was needed
- Finalize the report after conversations with participants
- Ensure a copy is placed in the student's permanent file

When leaders help teachers to be sure they know the rules and regulations that govern these procedures in their school, they become experts on exactly what they are responsible for, and the teachers can figure out the best way to use the evaluation and reporting process to support student learning. It is well worth taking this time.

A clear and established process is important to ensure that the job of reporting is being done properly. For example:

One principal asks teachers to submit comprehensive collections of student evidence for *one student* each term, along with report cards for every student in the class. He reviews the evidence for that student, speaking with the teacher if questions emerge, reads all report cards, and signs them when they are finalized. Sometimes the reports have simple typographical errors that need to be corrected. Other times the errors are much more significant. Prior to signing reports, all errors must be corrected.

Another principal, concerned with the lack of knowledge around the electronic grading program, has the technology support person available during professional learning times devoted to issues related to grading. Once staff agreements regarding appropriate grading practices (given district policy and regulations) have been reached, this expert helps teachers refine the grading program to suit their reporting needs. The principal meets with every teacher over the course of the year to ensure that their grading and reporting practices match current policy. The technology person assists in problem solving any issues that emerge so that inappropriate or misinformed use of technology in regards to reporting doesn't put teachers (and students) at risk.

Some schools have structured their reporting periods to allow for the student-parent-teacher conference to precede the writing of the report card. During the conference time, students provide evidence of their learning through the demonstration of performance tasks and by sharing portfolios of their work. Conversations include a clear focus on areas of strength and improvement. The report card follows a couple of weeks later and serves as a synopsis of what was discussed and observed during the conference. Teachers who have experience with this structure note an increase in parent attendance and participation. Since parents do not have a report card in hand prior to the conference, they view that time as critical to find out important information about their child's learning.

When examining current practices regarding reporting, it is essential that the policy, regulations, and in-school agreements be clear and applied uniformly. Procedures must be in place to ensure reporting is conducted properly and to protect those writing student reports from being at risk.

Supporting Classroom Teachers

One way we can support classroom teachers is through this process of clarification, training, and supervision of the reporting process. A powerful starting point is to have teachers read chapter 10 in *Making Classroom Assessment Work* and take time to complete the end-of-chapter tasks (shown on the following page). Another resource, *Assessment* of *Learning: Standards-Based Grading and Reporting* (Davies 2008), has also proven helpful to leaders as it provides a full-day workshop as well as responses to many frequently asked questions.

Guiding Our Own Learning

Begin planning for your reporting process:

- Search out copies of relevant documents and regulations with regards to reporting. Be clear about what you must do.
- Record any definitions currently in place for summative symbols, such as grades or marks and numbers.
- Think about how to expand the definitions so as to include more information about learning and the qualities likely to be apparent in the evidence if students have learned well.
- Create your own description of achievement for one course or subject area, modeled after the examples in this chapter. Ask a colleague to review it. When you are confident that it accurately describes what students are expected to know, be able to do, and articulate, share it with one group of students. Try it out. Modify and refine it until you are comfortable enough to share it with other students and their parents.

Guiding the Learning of Students

As you prepare students to self-assess their way to success, share the description of achievement for one term with them. Ask students to build a list of possible evidence with you. Record all their ideas. Add your own.

Periodically ask students to collect evidence of their learning in relation to the description of achievement. Then, as reporting time draws near, have them finalize their collection of evidence and present it to you, along with a self-report that describes how well they have learned and what they need to learn next. Remind students to attach proof—a piece of evidence—to each statement they make. When students are ready, have them present their evidence to you, and if they are prepared, to others.

This one change, from *teachers* being accountable to *students* being accountable, can make a huge difference in who is seen as responsible for learning. Students need to assume ownership for their learning.

From © 2011 *Making Classroom Assessment Work* (3rd edition) by Anne Davies, p. 104

If this process is new to you and your school, proceed *slowly*. Quality reporting cannot be a hit-and-miss venture in these times. One way to begin is to engage teachers in creating their own description of achievement for one course or subject area, modeled after the examples in chapter 3. Have them work with colleagues to review and improve it. When they are confident that it accurately describes what students are expected to know, be able to do, and articulate, have them share it with one group of students. They need to try it out and refine it until they are comfortable enough to share it with all students and their parents.

As teachers prepare students to self-assess their way to success, they share the description of achievement for one term with them. They ask students to build a list of possible evidence together with them. Consider the following task from *Making Classroom Assessment Work* (p. 104). Periodically, they ask students to collect evidence of their learning in relation to the description of achievement. Then, as reporting time draws near, they have students finalize their collection of evidence and present it to them, along with a self-report that describes how well the students feel they are learning. Teachers remind students to attach proof—a piece of evidence—to each statement they make. When students are ready, they present their evidence to teachers, and if they are prepared, to others. This one change—from *teachers* being accountable to *students* being accountable—can make a huge difference in who is seen as responsible for learning (Davies 2011). What might this mean for you in your leadership role?

Being a Lead Learner

The process of evaluation and reporting is not easy. Lead learners come to understand that more fully when we begin to implement similar practices in our work. Every time we evaluate classroom teachers, we have an opportunity to model good assessment, evaluation, and reporting practices. Consider supervision responsibilities. How could you align those with the way teachers are now being asked to report and evaluate? Use the following questions as a guide:

- Are you working within the legal requirements for evaluation and reporting in this school and district?
- Have you developed an assessment plan for each program or job you are supervising?
- Do you have an approved description of what success looks like?

Have you defined, in qualitative as well as quantitative terms, the meaning of each symbol?

- How are the adult learners involved in the assessment process?
- Are you collecting samples of growth over time? Do learners have multiple opportunities to learn? Can they show what they know in a variety of ways?
- Are adult learners involved in collecting and organizing the evidence?
- What evidence do you examine, and how do you evaluate evidence of adult learning or program success in preparation for reporting?
- Do adult learners understand what they are to learn and how you will evaluate? Do they have an opportunity to question your evaluation prior to reports being filed?
- Is there an opportunity for others to review the evidence of learning and provide feedback to the learner prior to evaluating and reporting?
- Is there an opportunity for the adult learners and you to meet and discuss strengths and areas needing improvement, and to set goals?
- Are adult learners informed if there are any perceived problems during the supervision process? Do they have time to learn?
- Are reports reviewed by another colleague or signed off by an administrative staff member (principal or vice principal) prior to being sent to the adult learner and filed?
- Are reports with signatures properly filed in the learner's permanent file?

Reporting indicators vary from place to place. You will need to develop your own list according to your own context. On pages 122 and 123, a chart called Evaluation and Reporting provides a 12-step overview of leaders' responsibilities, given that they need to inform teachers, support teachers, and use appropriate practices themselves.

In view of the increase in litigation, this process protects teachers as well as educational leaders. Once staff has reviewed the agreed-upon procedures, it is the administrative team's job to ensure everything is done as required. Leaders must:

- Inform teachers of the rules and regulations concerning evaluation and reporting
- Support teachers to do quality work in this area
- Assess and evaluate teachers in relation to student learning, teaching, assessment, and evaluation

Another way lead learners engage in reporting and evaluation is in their reports on the progress toward school or district goals or plans. In this case, the audience may be the community, state, or provincial education departments. A sample outline for superintendents (the Reviewing Reporting Process) is seen below.

Reviewing Reporting Process

Questions to Consider	Notes
Are you working within the legal requirements for evaluation and reporting to community and/or state/provincial education authorities?	
Have you developed an assessment plan for each school or district goal/priority?	
Do you have a collaboratively developed description of what success looks like?	
How is your staff involved in the assessment process?	
Are you collecting evidence over time so that growth can be noted along the way and, if necessary, adjustments can be made?	
How is your staff involved in collecting and organizing the evidence? Have responsibilities been assigned to various members of your team?	
What evidence does your team examine, and how do you evaluate evidence of results against your stated goals, in preparation for reporting?	
Do your immediate staff and others in your school/system understand what is being evaluated?	
Are reports written in language that educational partners can understand?	
How do you share the reports and results both within and outside the school/district?	
Do you include information regarding gaps or problems that have been identified through the collection of evidence?	

The Reviewing Reporting Process outline can be found as a reproducible on page 169 of appendix 2.

Leading the Way: Evaluation and Reporting

	Leaders *Informing* Teachers	Leaders *Supporting* Teachers	Leaders *Assessing and Evaluating* Teachers/Others
1.	Have legal requirements been shared and discussed? Have emerging problems been solved, and have the solutions been brought back to the entire staff? Has the impact of these requirements on classroom practices been discussed?	Are you providing feedback to teachers on how well they are working within the legal requirements for reporting in this school and district?	Are you following due process for teacher evaluation as outlined by policy?
2.	Have you communicated that assessment plans should include the learning destination (based on relevant standards or learning outcomes), the evidence of learning to be collected, and samples that show quality is developed, submitted, and reviewed early in the year?	Are you leading teachers through questions such as "Have you developed an assessment plan for each course or subject area?"	Have you developed an assessment plan for teacher/staff evaluations that includes evidence from a variety of sources?
3.	Are expectations that the method for evaluating evidence of learning, prior to reporting, detailed and available to students and parents, as well as principals and teachers?	Are you providing feedback to teachers in terms of whether they have an approved description of what success looks like? Are you encouraging them to define in qualitative, as well as quantitative, terms the meaning of each report card symbol?	Do you have a learning destination for effective teaching, assessment, and evaluation? Have you developed criteria with the teachers you will be evaluating?
4.	Have you discussed the importance of assessment *for* learning, the commitment to ensuring all students learn, and a plan for increasing student motivation, engagement, and ownership?	How are you helping teachers involve students in the classroom assessment process? How are you modeling this?	How are teachers involved in the assessment and evaluation process of their own practice?
5.	Are you stressing that students have time to learn, by themselves and with others? Are you informing teachers that students learn and submit work, get specific, descriptive feedback, and then improve their work as they learn more?	How are you supporting teachers to collect samples of growth over time and to provide students with multiple opportunities to learn and show what they know in a variety of ways?	Are teachers using samples of effective teaching, assessment, and evaluation? Do they have multiple opportunities to learn and demonstrate their growing expertise? Can they show what they know in a variety of ways?
6.	Do all teachers understand that students are expected to collect evidence of their learning from a variety of sources, which is defined as more than grades or marks?	How are you supporting teachers as they engage students in collecting and organizing evidence?	How are teachers involved in collecting and organizing the evidence of their teaching practice?

Leading the Way: Evaluation and Reporting (page 2)

7.	Have you encouraged teachers to create a plan for evaluating student work and to review collections of student work with colleagues? Are there procedures in place to ensure that they are valuing the work the way others would? That is, scoring bodies of student work against criteria and checking to see colleagues are scoring and marking student work in similar ways (inter-rater reliability).	What structures have you put in place to allow teachers to evaluate evidence of student learning in preparation for reporting?	What is included in the body of evidence you examine regarding teacher performance? Does it come from multiple sources? How will you evaluate it in preparation for reporting?
8.	Have you asked teachers to make explicit (in writing) course goals, the evidence of learning that will be required, and how marks or grades will be determined? Do they understand that when their evaluation is complete, students need to have an opportunity to review it and ask questions?	What structures or collaborative meeting times have you organized to support teachers in developing course goals and evaluation plans? How do you facilitate communication between teacher and student, and teacher and homes? Do students have an opportunity to question teachers' evaluations prior to reports going home?	Do teachers understand what they are to know, to do, and be able to articulate? Do they know how you will evaluate? Do they have an opportunity to question your evaluation prior to your final report?
9.	Do parents receive copies of the course outline and evaluation process? Are they able to review progress on an ongoing basis whether that is online, through work samples sent home, or in person? Are teachers aware that parents must have an opportunity to review student work during the term and prior to reports going home?	What structures are put in place for parents to review the evidence of learning and provide feedback to the student, prior to reporting?	Is there an opportunity for the teacher to involve others in collecting and reviewing the evidence of learning and provide feedback?
10.	Have you discussed the value of inviting parents to meet with the teacher and the student to review student work and discuss next learning steps?	What time has been set aside for parents, students, and teachers to meet and discuss strengths, areas needing improvement, and goals? How do you connect, engage, and support your teachers in connecting with parents who find it difficult to communicate with the school?	Is there an opportunity for you to meet with the teachers, prior to beginning your evaluation and completing your report, to discuss strengths and areas needing improvement, and to set goals?
11.	Do teachers contact parents before reporting periods when it appears a student is not learning successfully? Are school administrators regularly informed regarding students at risk?	What structures and processes have you put in place to dialogue about the learning profiles of students and to communicate students' needs to parents?	Are teachers notified if there is a problem with learning in their classroom? Are they given an opportunity to receive specific, descriptive feedback and to be coached towards success?
12.	Is it established that all reports are reviewed and signed by a school administrator prior to being sent home, and a copy, with signature, filed in the student's permanent file?	Are reports reviewed by another colleague or signed off by an administrative staff member (principal or vice principal) prior to being sent home?	Is the draft report and accompanying evidence reviewed by another colleague prior to being finalized? Are final reports on teacher performance signed, properly submitted, and filed?

page 2 of 2

Planning to Walk the Talk

Take some time to review the policies and procedures with regards to reporting. Consider what must be done now and what changes are needed to bring policies and procedures into alignment with quality classroom assessment practices—both assessment *for* learning and assessment *of* learning. Make notes. Begin a discussion with your leadership team. Plan to spend time researching, learning, and reflecting, prior to taking action. Moving too quickly or too slowly can do more harm than good. Consider placing your notes in your draft portfolio collection.

Learning by Ourselves and With Others

"Much of the process of education consists of being able to distance oneself in some way from what one knows by being able to reflect on one's own knowledge."

Jerome Bruner

Contents

Learning to make assessment work is an ongoing task. Keeping ourselves learning and on track can be a challenge in our busy lives. One approach learners find helpful is to be part of a group of people learning together. These days, most educators refer to these groups as *learning teams* or *professional learning communities*. Another favorite term is *learning circles*—places where people learn from each other.

When we learn together, we share experiences that help us understand our thinking. This helps us grow and develop at our own pace. Sometimes *belonging* means following structured protocols to deepen our learning in certain, deliberate ways. Other times, the learning circle's journey is more evolutionary. As members of a learning group, we can access the support we need to take risks, or to prevent us from leaping without a parachute.

Your Learning Circle

You probably already belong to more than one learning circle. Some may be formally established and part of your job. Others are adopted or created by you. Some will last for months and others, for years. We are learning all the time—by talking with others about what we are trying, by sharing books, websites, and blogs that are helping us learn, or by calling someone to share a success or get advice. We know that sometimes we need to learn by ourselves and sometimes, we need input from others. At those times, friends and colleagues can help us realize what we know and what we want to learn more about.

Educators as Learners and Researchers

To be effective, learning circles must be implemented in ways that are respectful of adults as learners. When participants are invited to be involved and when they choose what and how they are going to learn, the power of their learning can be astonishing.

Sometimes potential participants choose not to accept the invitation to learn about and research classroom assessment. It may be that they are not ready to explore this process at their stage of development. At the same time, they might offer insights and helpful suggestions on ways to create a learning circle that is more accessible and supportive to all learners. Be willing to listen and plan accordingly.

We need to remember that we all learn in different ways and at different rates. When we treat our colleagues with respect, and when we provide a variety of learning experiences, we begin to build a safe learning environment. Ask colleagues for ideas about what kind of support they need to meet their professional goals. Unless adults feel safe enough to take the risks necessary to learn, change will never happen. Go slowly. A destination can be achieved by many varied routes.

Guidelines to Consider

Here are some guidelines that might help you form a learning circle: *Start small, get organized together,* and *share responsibility.*

Start small. Begin with a few people you think might be interested in learning more about supporting student learning through assessment. Draw up a list of people, and call them to arrange a time to get together for a first gathering. Even one other person is a good start. As time passes, you will find other kindred spirits to join you. Your learning circle can begin by sharing favorite assessment resources or by having participants tell their own assessment stories. Invite participants to describe incidents that caused them to become interested in improving classroom assessment for their students. Listen to each other and ask questions. Find out if there are common threads of experience. Look for shared interests within the field of classroom assessment.

Get organized together. Acting as a leader for the first gathering, explain your vision for the group. Briefly touch on the following issues:

- Name the reasons for starting a group.
- Decide what the group might do or accomplish.
- Consider whether it will be more like a book club, a time to share successful classroom assessment ideas, or a combination of both.
- Discuss whether or not you are going to use a book (this one or another) as a guide.
- Develop a plan for where and how often the group might meet.
- Talk about how each gathering could proceed and be organized.

After you share your ideas, ask participants to share theirs. Feel your way, through conversation, toward a final agreement on these issues. Avoid being overly ambitious. The more obligations you put on yourselves, the less likely they will be fulfilled. Consider meeting once a month rather than biweekly. Consider skipping particularly busy months.

Share responsibility. Each meeting should be conducted by someone who's been designated in advance. This might be the group leader, the person hosting the meeting, or a volunteer. The organizer needs to make sure everyone is reminded about the upcoming meeting and must be prepared to devise alternative plans if necessary. A facilitator is also needed to keep the meeting on track by ensuring that everyone has a chance to contribute and that an agreed-upon structure is followed. (See page 128 for sample Learning Circle guidelines.)

Learning by Ourselves and With Colleagues

We can learn by ourselves, with our grade-level or department colleagues, with a school faculty, across a family of schools, or across a large professional group of educators.

This book is designed to deepen your understanding of classroom assessment and to demonstrate ways to lead others toward better quality assessment practices.

You could also consider introducing your colleagues to *Making Classroom Assessment Work* using the structured conversation on the opposite page.

Advice From Learning Circles

- Be respectful of each other.

- Agree that being a professional means adapting, not adopting, new ideas.

- Agree that there are lots of right ways to teach, assess, and learn.

- Ask thoughtful questions.

- Welcome all points of view.

- Limit the frequency and length of meetings.

- Agree how participants will take turns talking.

- Agree to give each speaker undivided attention without interrupting.

- Agree to refrain from giving advice or ideas unless the speaker requests them.

- Agree that conversations at the meeting should not be repeated elsewhere unless permission is granted by the person sharing the story.

Learning With Our Department or Grade-Level Colleagues

Creating a learning circle of your grade level or department colleagues and sharing your work related to classroom assessment will help you benefit from your colleagues' expertise and give you someone with whom to try out your ideas.

Structured Conversation to Be Used With
Making Classroom Assessment Work

Learning Goal:

The purpose of this session is to focus participants on the elements of comprehensive classroom assessment and give them an overview of the entire process. It is also designed to help participants formulate questions to guide their own reading of the text and their conversations with one another.

Materials:

Making Classroom Assessment Work for each participant; chart paper for sharing and listing of questions

Getting Started:

1. Explain that the purpose of classroom assessment is to support student learning and also to communicate evidence of that learning to others.
2. Acknowledge that we all have different ways and use different strategies to assess student learning. We use the assessment information we gather to support the different learning needs of students.
3. Note that one of our jobs as professionals is to learn about assessment and thought-fully select a set of ideas and strategies that make sense for the students in our school community.
4. Then, number off the participants from one to ten, and ask them to read one chapter in *Making Classroom Assessment Work*, so that each chapter is read by one or more people.
5. As they read, participants should note two or three ideas that capture the message of the chapter and form one question about it. If participants finish early, encourage them to browse the other chapters.
6. Arrange participants into "expert groups" (1s together, 2s together, and so on) to discuss their findings and questions.
7. Rearrange participants into groups of one to ten. Invite them to talk about the big picture of classroom assessment. Ask one person to record questions that arise.

Debriefing the Learning:

As a large group, record the questions that have arisen. Invite participants to use these questions to focus subsequent learning conversations.

Taking Action:

Choose one or more:
- Encourage participants to read the rest of the book and generate more questions.
- Invite participants to work independently on the Guiding Your Own Learning at the end of each chapter.
- Decide the next steps in exploring classroom assessment.

Learning Across Our School

Some schools have chosen to use *Making Classroom Assessment Work* as an applied book study, in which educators work by themselves, with grade-level or department colleagues, and then across grades or departments, in order to build a comprehensive schoolwide approach to classroom assessment. This schoolwide dialogue allows teachers to build upon the experiences students have in other classes, thereby building a common language between students, teachers, and over time, parents. In some places, groups of schools have gathered to extend the conversation across buildings, so that families of schools (elementary to middle to secondary) have a common language and set of experiences upon which to build.

Learning Across Many Schools

Educators who are engaged in professional development as part of a larger jurisdiction have used a variety of resources, including *Making Classroom Assessment Work*, to support ongoing learning about classroom assessment.

Remember that learning circles are powerful circles of friends (or soon-to-be friends) learning together. They arise out of common interests and a willingness to share the journey with others. They last as long as they work, coming in and out of existence, as people pose questions and answer them.

Planning to Walk the Talk

Consider how you best learn. Ask others how their learning is best supported. It helps to provide a variety of learning opportunities—no size fits all. Plan to meet the diverse learning needs of adults through a range of learning opportunities that allow for choice.

"At first they said it couldn't be done but some were doing it. Then they said it could only be done by a few under special conditions, but more were doing it. Then they said, 'Why would you do it any other way?'"

Anonymous

Final Thoughts

"If you want to build a ship, don't drum up people together to collect wood and don't assign them tasks and work, but rather teach them to long for the endless immensity of the sea."

Antoine de Saint-Exupéry

Leading the way involves blazing a trail for others while holding the vision of the desired destination. Leaders must rise above the trivial problems, oversee the needs of the whole group, and keep a high perspective in order to inspire others to follow.

Life on the mountaintops can be challenging and lonely at times for lead learners. By using these assessment techniques, the work and excitement of learning together becomes a shared journey. Once we are on our way, keeping on track can be simple. It requires the following steps:

1. Keep our focus on that which is most important—students and their learning.
2. Stay informed and involve everyone in providing feedback, so that necessary adjustments can be made throughout the process.
3. Celebrate our successes.

As we incorporate assessment *for* learning into our daily routines, colleagues and students will become more adept at taking charge of their own education.

The companion book to this one for leaders is called *Transforming Schools and Systems Using Assessment: A Practical Guide.* Our journey as lead learners challenges us to engage our system—whether this is a small team, a department, an entire school, a district, board, or jurisdiction—in educational change. Assessment *for* learning can serve as both the content and the lens of the change. Filled with practical examples and lessons from those who have tried and succeeded, this book equips us for our new adventure.

" *A good leader inspires people to have confidence in the leader; a great leader inspires people to have confidence in themselves.* **"**

Anonymous

Acknowledgments

A book such as this is only ever accomplished as a result of walking and learning alongside others. Together, these experiences have helped us help find our way. We thank those students and classroom teachers who have welcomed us into their classrooms, and we stand in awe of school and district leaders who have risked doing the right work, day after day.

This series has had a wonderful production team—we would like to thank Ken Chong, Mackenzie Duncan, Kelly Giordano, Judith Hall-Patch, Annie Jack, Cori Jones, and Lynn Nichol. Each of you, in your own way, has made it all possible.

On closing, we are mindful that who we are professionally reflects who we are personally. We wish to express our heartfelt love and appreciation to those people in our lives who make life worth living—our colleagues, our friends, our families. We wish you blessings along your journey.

We'd like to thank the Solution Tree team, particularly Douglas Rife and Gretchen Knapp, for their vision, support, and hard work.

Anne, Sandra, and Beth
August 2011

References

Andrade, H. 2011. Foreword. In K. Gregory, C. Cameron, and A. Davies *Self-Assessment and Goal Setting*, 2nd Edition (pp. 7–16). Bloomington, IN: Solution Tree Press.

Anthony, R., T. Johnson, N. Mickelson, and A. Preece. 1991. *Evaluating Literacy: A Perspective for Change*. Portsmouth, NH: Heinemann.

Aronson, E. 1972. *The Social Animal*. New York: Viking.

Assessment Reform Group (ARG). 2005. ARG-ASF Project, Working Papers 1-4. Assessment systems for the future: the place of assessment by teachers. http://k1.ioe.ac.uk/tlrp/arg/ASF.html

Assessment Reform Group (ARG). 2006. *The Role of Teachers in the Assessment of Learning*. Pamphlet produced by Assessment Systems for the Future project (ASF). Retrieved November 8, 2011 from http://arrts.gtcni.org.uk/gtcni/handle/2428/4617

Barlow, M. and H. Robertson. 1994. *Class Warfare*. Toronto, ON: Key Porter Books.

BC Ministry of Education. 1990. *Primary Program Foundation Document*. Victoria, BC: Queens' Printer.

BC Ministry of Education. 2000. *Primary Program: A Framework for Teaching*. Victoria, BC: Queens' Printer.

Berliner, D. and B. Biddle. 1998. *The Manufactured Crisis: Myths, Frauds and the Attack on America's Public Schools*. New York: Longman.

Bibby, R. W. and D. C. Posterski. 1992. *Teen Trends: A Nation in Motion*. Toronto, ON: Stoddart Press.

Black, P. and D. Wiliam. 1998. Inside the black box: Raising standards through classroom assessment. *Phi Delta Kappan* 80, no. 2: 1–20.

Black, P. and D. Wiliam. 1998. Assessment and classroom learning. *Assessment in Education* 5, no. 1: 7–75.

Boud, D. 1995. *Enhancing Learning Through Self-Assessment*. London, UK: Kogan Page.

Brookhart, S. 2001. Successful students' formative and summative uses of assessment information. *Assessment in Education* 8, no. 21: 153–169.

Brooks, J. and M. Brooks. 1993. *In Search of Understanding: The Case for Constructivist Classrooms*. Alexandria, VA: ASCD.

Brown, J. and E. Langer. 1990. Mindfulness and intelligence: A comparison. *Educational Psychologist* 25, no. 3–4: 305–335.

Bruner, J. 1986. *Actual Minds, Possible Worlds*. Cambridge, MA: Harvard University Press.

Burger, J., C. F. Webber, and P. Klinck (Eds.). 2007. *Intelligent Leadership: Constructs for Thinking Education Leaders*. New York: Kluwer Academic Publishers.

Butler, R. 1987. Task-involving and ego-involving properties of evaluation: Effects of different feedback conditions on motivational perceptions, interest and performance. *Journal of Educational Psychology* 79, no. 4: 474–482.

Butler, R. 1988. Enhancing and undermining intrinsic motivation: The effects of task-involving and ego-involving evaluation on interest and performance. *British Journal of Educational Psychology* 58: 1–14.

Butler, R. and M. Nisan. 1986. Effects of no feedback, task-related comments and grades on intrinsic motivation and performance. *Journal of Educational Psychology* 78, no. 3: 210–216.

Butterworth, R. W. and W. B. Michael. 1975. The relationship of reading achievement, school attitude, and self-responsibility behaviors of sixth grade pupils to comparative and individuated reporting systems: Implication of improvement of validity of the evaluation and pupil performance. *Educational and Psychological Measurement* 35: 987–991.

Calkins, L. 1991. *Living Between the Lines*. Portsmouth, NH: Heinemann.

Cantalini, M. 1987. *The Effects of Age and Gender on School Readiness and School Success*. Unpublished doctoral dissertation. Toronto, ON: OISE.

Ceci, S. J. 1990. *On Intelligence—More or Less: A Bio-Ecological Treatise on Intellectual Development*. Englewood Cliffs, NJ: Prentice Hall.

Centre for Educational Research and Innovation. 2005. *Formative Assessment—Improving Learning in Secondary Classrooms*. London, UK: OECD.

Cicourel, A., K. W. Jennings, S. H. M. Jennings, K. C. W. Leiter, R. MacKay, H. Mehan, and D. R. Roth (Eds.). 1974. *Language Use and School Performance*. New York: Academic Press.

Covington, M. V. 1998. *The Will to Learn: A Guide for Motivating Young People*. Cambridge, UK: Cambridge University Press.

Crooks, T. 1988. *Assessing Student Performance*. New South Wales, AUS: Higher Education Research and Developing Society of Australasia.

Crooks, T. 1988. The impact of classroom evaluation on students. *Review of Educational Research* 58, no. 4: 438–481.

Csikszentmihalyi, M. 1993. *The Evolving Self: A Psychology for the Third Millennium*. New York: HarperCollins.

Curwin, R. 1978. The grades of wrath: Some alternatives. *Learning* 6, no. 6: 60–64.

Davies, A. 2004. *Facilitator's Guide to Classroom Assessment K–12* (Multimedia resource). Courtenay, BC: Connections Publishing.

Davies, A. 2004. *Finding Proof of Learning in a One-to-One Computing Classroom*. Courtenay, BC: Connections Publishing.

Davies, A. 2008. *Assessment of Learning: A Professional Learning Resource on Standards-Based Grading and Reporting*. (Multimedia resource). Courtenay, BC: Connections Publishing.

Davies, A. 2011. *Making Classroom Assessment Work,* 3rd Edition. Bloomington, IN: Solution Tree Press.

Davies, A., C. Cameron, C. Politano, and K. Gregory. 1992. *Together Is Better: Collaborative Assessment, Evaluation, and Reporting*. Winnipeg, MB: Peguis Publishers.

DeCharms, R. 1968. *Personal Causation: The Internal Affective Determinants of Behavior*. New York: Academic Press.

DeCharms, R. 1972. Personal causation training in schools. *Journal of Applied Social Psychology* 2: 95–113.

Deci, E. and R. M. Ryan. 1985. *Intrinsic Motivation and Self-Determination in Human Behavior*. New York: Plenum Press.

Deci, E. and R. M. Ryan. 2002. *Handbook of Self-Determination Research*. Rochester, NY: University of Rochester Press.

Deverell, R. S. 1994. Interview with Peter Gzowski, CBC Radio *Morningside* show.

Dewey, J. 1933. *How We Think: A Restatement of the Relation of Reflective Thinking to the Educative Process*. Lexington, MA: Heath.

Dixon, N., A. Davies, and C. Politano. 1996. *Learning With Readers Theatre.* Winnipeg, MB: Peguis Publishers.

Doidge, N. 2007. *The Brain That Changes Itself: Stories of Personal Triumph From the Frontiers of Brain Science.* London: Penguin Books.

Dornbusch, S. 1994. School tracking harms millions, sociologist finds. *Stanford University News Service.* March 2, 1994. Retrieved November 8, 2011, from http://www.stanford.edu/dept/news /pr/94/940302Arc4396.html.

Drummond, M. J. 1994. *Learning to See: Assessment Through Observation.* Markham, ON: Pembroke Publishers.

Dweck, C. S. 2000. *Self-Theories: Their Role in Motivation, Personality and Development.* Philadelphia: Psychology Press.

Elbow, P. 1986. *Embracing Contraries: Explorations in Learning and Teaching.* New York: Oxford University Press.

Ellis, J. 1968. *The Effects of Same Sex Class Organization of Junior High School Students' Academic Achievement, Self-Discipline, Self-Concept, Sex-Role Identification and Attitudes Toward School.* Washington, DC: US Department of Health, Education, and Welfare.

Ericsson, K. A., R. T. Krampe, and C. Tesch-Rome. 1993. The role of deliberate practice in the acquisition of expert performance. *Psychological Review* 100, no. 3: 363–406.

Erickson, H. L. 1998. *Concept-Based Curriculum and Instruction: Teaching Beyond the Facts.* Thousand Oaks, CA: Corwin Press.

Fullan, M. 2001. Keynote presentation. Principals and Vice-Principals Conference, Victoria, BC, Canada.

Funk, H. D. 1969. Non-promotion teaches children they are inferior. *Education Digest* 35, no. 3: 38–39.

Gardner, H. 1984. *Frames of Mind: The Theory of Multiple Intelligences.* New York: Basic Books.

Gardner, J. (Ed.). 2005. *Assessment and Learning.* Thousand Oaks, CA: SAGE.

Gazzaniga, M. 1992. *Nature's Mind: The Biological Roots of Thinking, Emotions, Sexuality, Language, and Intelligence.* New York: Basic Books.

Gearhardt, M. and S. Wolf. 1995. *Teachers' and Students' Roles in Large-Scale Portfolio Assessment: Providing Evidence of Competency With the Purpose and Processes of Writing.* Los Angeles: UCLA/CRESST.

Gibbs, C. and G. Stobart. 1993. *Assessment: A Teacher's Guide to the Issues,* 2nd Edition. Oxford, UK: Hodder and Stoughton.

Glaude, C. 2011. *Protocols for Professional Learning Conversations.* Bloomington, IN: Solution Tree Press.

Glaude, C. 2011. *When Students Fail to Learn.* Bloomington, IN: Solution Tree Press.

Goleman, D. 1996. *Emotional Intelligence: Why It Can Matter More Than IQ.* New York: Bantam Books.

Gould, S. J. 1981. *The Mismeasure of Man.* New York: Norton.

Gredler, G. R. 1984. Transition classes: A viable alternative to the at-risk child. *Psychology in the Schools* 21, no. 4: 463–470.

Gregory, K., C. Cameron, and A. Davies. 2011. *Conferencing and Reporting,* 2nd Edition. Bloomington, IN: Solution Tree Press.

Gregory, K., C. Cameron, and A. Davies. 2011. *Self-Assessment and Goal-Setting,* 2nd Edition. Bloomington, IN: Solution Tree Press.

Gregory, K., C. Cameron, and A. Davies. 2011. *Setting and Using Criteria,* 2nd Edition. Bloomington, IN: Solution Tree Press.

Harlen, W. 2006. *The Role of Teachers in the Assessment of Learning.* Pamphlet produced by Assessment Systems for the Future project (ASF) Assessment Reform Group, UK.

Harlen, W. and R. Deakin Crick. 2002. *Testing, Motivation and Learning.* Booklet produced by Assessment Reform Group at University of Cambridge Faculty of Education.

Harlen, W. and R. Deakin Crick. 2003. Testing and motivation for learning. *Assessment in Education* 10, no. 2: 169–208.

Harter, S. 1978. Pleasure derived from challenge and the effects of receiving grades on children's difficulty level choices. *Child Development* 49, no. 3: 788–799.

Hattie, J. 1992. *What Works in Special Education.* Presentation to the Special Education Conference, May 1992. Retrieved September 15, 2011, from http://www.education.auckland.ac.nz/webdav/site/education/shared/hattie/docs/special-education.pdf.

Hattie, J. 2008. *Visible Learning: A Synthesis of Over 800 Meta-Analyses Relating to Achievement.* New York: Routledge.

Hattie, J. and H. Timperley. 2007. The power of feedback. *Review of Educational Research 77,* no. 1: 81–112.

Healy, J. 1990. *Endangered Minds.* New York: Touchstone.

Henderson, A. T. and N. Berla (Eds.). 1994. *A New Generation of Evidence: The Family Is Critical to Student Achievement.* Washington, DC: National Committee for Citizens in Education.

Hill, J., T. C. Reeves, M. Grant, S-K. Wang, and S. Wan. 2002. *The Impact of Portable Technologies on Teaching and Learning. Year Three Report.* Paper presented at the annual meeting of the American Educational Research Association, New Orleans. Retrieved September 11, 2003, from http://lpsl.coe.uga.edu/projects/aalaptop/pdf/aa3rd/Year3ReportFinalVersion.pdf.

Hillocks, G. 1986. *Research on Written Composition.* Champaign, IL: NCTE.

Hoffer, E. 1973. *Reflections on the Human Condition.* New York: Harper-Collins.

Holmes, C. T. 1989. Grade level retention effects: A meta-analysis of research studies. In L. A. Shepard and M. L. Smith (Eds.) *Flunking Grades: The Policies and Effects of Retention* (pp. 16–33). London, UK: Falmer Press.

Hurford, S. 1998. I can see clearly now—student learning profiles. *Primary Leadership* 1, no. 2: 22–29.

Jensen, E. 1998. *Teaching With the Brain in Mind.* Alexandria, VA: ASCD.

Jeroski, S. 2003. *Wireless Writing Project: School District No. 60 (Peace River North) Research Report: Phase II.* Vancouver, BC: Horizon Research & Evaluation, Inc.

Joslin, G. 2002. *Investigating the Influence of Rubric Assessment Practices on the Student's Desire to Learn.* Unpublished manuscript. San Diego State University.

Jovanovic, L. 1979. J. H. Sissons Staff Meeting, August, in Yellowknife, NWT.

Kohn, A. 1999. *Punished by Rewards: The Trouble With Gold Stars, Incentive Plans, A's, Praise, and Other Bribes.* Boston: Houghton Mifflin.

Kulik, J. A. and L. C. Kulik. 1992. Meta-analytic findings on grouping programs. *Gifted Child Quarterly* 36, no. 2: 73–77.

Kyle, J. 1992. *Literature Review: Letter Grades and Anecdotal Reporting.* Internal Working Document, Ministry of Education.

Laboratory Network Program. 1993. *A Tool Kit for Professional Developers: Alternative Assessment.* Portland, OR: Northwest Regional Educational Laboratory. Retrieved November 9, 2011, from http://apps.educationnorthwest.org/toolkit98/Act1-5.html.

Langer, E. J. 1997. *The Power of Mindful Learning.* Reading, MA: Addison-Wesley.

Langer, J. and A. Applebee. 1986. Reading and writing instruction: Toward a theory of teaching and learning. *Review of Research in Education* 13: 171–194.

Le Doux, J. 1996. *The Emotional Brain.* New York: Simon & Schuster.

Lepper, M. R. and D. Greene. 1974. Turning play into work: Effects of adult surveillance and extrinsic rewards on children's intrinsic motivation. *Journal of Personality and Social Psychology* 45, no. 4 (December): 1141–1145.

Lepper, M. R. and D. Greene (Eds.). 1978. *The Hidden Costs of Rewards: New Perspectives on the Psychology of Human Motivation.* Hillsdale, NJ: Lawrence Erlbaum.

Levine, M. 1993. *All Kinds of Minds.* Cambridge, MA: Educators Publishing Service.

Lieberman, M. and E. J. Langer. 1995. Mindfulness in the process of learning. In E. J. Langer (Ed.), *The Power of Mindful Learning.* Reading, MA: Addison Wesley.

Light, D., M. McDermott, and M. Honey. 2002. *The Impact of Ubiquitous Portable Technology on an Urban School—Project Hiller.* Center for Children and Technology. Retrieved September 12, 2003, from http://www2.edc.org/CCT/admin/publications/report/Hiller-Final.pdf.

Lincoln, Y. and E. Guba. 1984. *Naturalistic Inquiry.* Beverly Hills, CA: SAGE.

Lowther, D., S. Ross, and G. Morrison. 2001. *Evaluation of a Laptop Program: Successes and Recommendation.* Paper presented at the "Building on the Future" NECC 2001: National Educational Computing Conference Proceedings, Chicago, IL, June 25–27,

2001. Retrieved September 11, 2003, from home.earthlink. net/~anebl/lowther.pdf.

Marzano, R. J. 2000. *Transforming Classroom Grading*. Alexandria, VA: ASCD.

Marzano, R. J., D. J. Pickering, and J. E. Pollock. 2001. *Classroom Instruction That Works: Research-Based Strategies for Increasing Student Achievement*. Alexandria, VA: ASCD.

Mehan, H. 1973. Assessing children's language-using abilities. In J. M. Armer and A. S. Grimshaw (Eds.) *Methodological Issues in Comparative Sociological Research* (pp. 309–343). New York: John Wiley and Sons.

Meisels, S., S. Atkins-Burnett, Y. Xue, D. D. Bickel, and S. H. Son. 2003. Creating a system of accountability: The impact of instructional assessment on elementary children's achievement scores. *Educational Policy Analysis Archives* 11, no. 9. Retrieved September 19, 2004 from http://epaa.asu.edu/epaa/v11n9/.

Mitra, S. Retrieved November 8, 2011, from http://www.ted.com/speakers /sugata_mitra.html

Natriello, G. 1984. Problems in the evaluation of students and student disengagement from secondary schools. *Journal of Research and Development in Education* 17, no. 4: 14–24.

Niklason, L. B. 1987. Do certain groups of children profit from a grade retention? *Psychology in the Schools* 24, no. 4: 339–345.

Nye, K. 1999. Open house: Let the kids do it. *Primary Leadership* 2, no. 1: 26–27.

Oakes, J. 1985. *Keeping Track: How Schools Structure Inequality*. New Haven, CT: Yale University Press.

Overman, M. 1986. Student promotion and retention. *Phi Delta Kappan* 67, no. 8: 609–613.

Palincsar, A. S. 1986. Reciprocal teaching. In A. S. Palincsar, E. Cooper, and N. Klotz *Teaching Reading as Thinking*, VHS. Washington, DC: NAK Production Association for the ASCD.

Palincsar, A. S. and A. L. Brown. 1986. Interactive teaching to promote independent learning from text. *The Reading Teacher* 39, no. 8: 771–777.

Papert, S. 1980. *Mindstorms: Children, Computers, and Powerful Ideas.* New York: Basic Books.

Papert, S. 1999. *Diversity in Learning: A Vision for the New Millennium Parts 1 & 2,* Diversity Task Force, convened by Vice President Al Gore.

Peck, S. 1998. *The Road Less Traveled.* New York: Simon & Schuster.

Pert, C. 1999. *Molecules of Emotion: The Science Behind Mind-Body Medicine.* New York: Scribner.

Peterson, S. E., J. S. De Gracie, and C. R. Ayabe. 1987. A longitudinal study of the effects of retention/promotion on academic achievement. *American Educational Research Journal* 24, no. 1: 107–118.

Pinker, S. 1997. *How the Mind Works.* New York: HarperCollins.

Politano, C. and A. Davies. 1994. *Multi-Age and More.* Winnipeg, MB: Peguis Publishers.

Popham, W. J. 1993. Circumventing the high costs of authentic assessment. *Phi Delta Kappan* 74, no. 6: 470–473.

Preece, A. 1995. Self-evaluation: Making it matter. In A. Costa and B. Kallick (Eds.), *Assessment in the Learning Organization* (pp. 30–48). Alexandria, VA: ASCD.

Proschaska, J.O., C. DiClemente, and J. Norcross. 1994. *Changing for Good.* New York: HarperCollins.

Restak, R. 2003. *The New Brain: How the Modern Age Is Rewiring Your Mind.* New York: St. Martin's Press.

Rock, D. 2009. *Your Brain at Work.* New York: Harper Business.

Rockman, S. 2003. Learning from laptops. In Cable in the Classroom's *Threshold Magazine* (Fall 2003): pp. 24–28.

Rockman, S. et al. 2000. *A More Complex Issue: Laptop Use and Impact in the Context of Changing Home and School Access.* The third in a series of research studies on Microsoft's Anytime Anywhere Learning Program. Retrieved November 8, 2011, from http://www.rockman.com/projects/126.micro.aal/yr3_report.pdf.

Rodriguez, M. C. 2004. The role of classroom assessment in student performance on TIMSS. *Applied Measurement in Education* 17, no. 1: 1–24.

Rothman, R. 1995. *Measuring Up: Standards, Assessment and School Reform.* San Francisco: Jossey-Bass.

Russell, M., D. Bebell, J. Cowan, and M. Corbelli. April 2002. *An AlphaSmart for Each Student: Does Teaching and Learning Change With Full Access to Word Processors?* Retrieved August 26, 2003, from http://www.bc.edu/research/intasc/PDF/AlphaSmartEachStudent.pdf.

Sadler, D. R. 1989. Formative assessment and the design of instructional systems. *Instructional Science* 16, no. 2: 119–144.

Schmoker, M. 1996. *Results: The Key to Continuous Improvement.* Alexandria, VA: ASCD.

Schön, D. A. 1983. *The Reflective Practitioner.* New York: Basic Books.

Schön, D. A. 1990. *Educating the Reflective Practitioner.* San Francisco: Jossey-Bass.

Sergiovanni, T. 1994. *Building Communities in Schools.* San Francisco: Jossey-Bass.

Shepard, L. A. 1989. Why we need better assessments. *Educational Leadership* 46, no. 7: 4–9.

Shepard, L. A. 2000. The role of assessment in a learning culture. *Educational Researcher* 29, no. 7: 4–14.

Shepard, L. A. and M. L. Smith. 1986. Synthesis of research on school readiness and kindergarten retention. *Educational Leadership* 44: 78–86.

Shepard, L. A. and M. L. Smith. 1987. What doesn't work: Explaining policies of retention in the early grades. *Phi Delta Kappan* 69: 129–134.

Shepard, L. A. and M. L. Smith. 1989. *Flunking Grades: Research and Policies on Retention.* New York: Falmer Press.

Shute, V. 2008. Focus on formative feedback. *Review of Educational Research* 78, no 1: 153–189.

Silvernail, D. L. 2005. *Does Maine's Middle School Laptop Program Improve Learning? A Review of Evidence to Date.* Portland: University of Southern Maine, Center for Education Policy, Applied Research, and Evaluation. Retrieved November 9, 2011, from http://usm.maine.edu/sites/default/files/Center%20for%20Education%20Policy,%20Applied%20Research,%20and%20Evaluation/MLTI705.pdf.

Slavin, R. E. 1987. Ability grouping and student achievement in elementary schools: A best-evidence synthesis. *Review of Educational Research* 57, no. 3: 293–336.

Slavin, R. E. 1990. Achievement effects of ability grouping in secondary schools: A best-evidence synthesis. *Review of Educational Research* 60, no. 3: 471–499.

Slavin, R. E. 1996. Research for the future: Research on cooperative learning and achievement: What we know, what we need to know. *Contemporary Educational Psychology* 21: 43–69.

Smith, A. and A. Davies. 1996. *Wordsmithing: A Spelling Program for Grades 3–8*. Winnipeg, MB: Peguis Publishers.

Smith, F. 1986. *Insult to Intelligence: The Bureaucratic Invasion of Our Classrooms*. Portsmouth, NH: Heinemann.

Springer, L., M. E. Stanne, and S. S. Donovan. 1999. Effects of small-group learning on undergraduates in science, mathematics, engineering, and technology: A meta-analysis. *Review of Educational Research* 69, no. 1: 21–51.

Sternberg, R. J. 1986. *Intelligence Applied: Understanding and Increasing Your Intellectual Skills*. San Diego: Harcourt Brace Jovanovich.

Sternberg, R. 1996. *Successful Intelligence: How Practical and Creative Intelligence Determines Success in Life*. New York: Simon & Schuster.

Stiggins, R. 2004. *Student-Involved Assessment for Learning*, 4th Edition. Upper Saddle River, NJ: Pearson Prentice Hall.

Stiggins, R. 2007. Assessment through the student's eyes. *Educational Leadership* 64, no. 8: 22–26.

Sylwester, R. 1995. *A Celebration of Neurons: An Educator's Guide to the Brain*. Alexandria, VA: ASCD.

Thome, C. C. 2001. *The Effects of Classroom-Based Assessment Using an Analytical Writing Rubric on High School Students' Writing Achievement*. Cardinal Stritch University. Unpublished Dissertation.

Tieso, C. L. 2003. Ability grouping is not just tracking anymore. *Roeper Review* 26: 29–36.

Tomlinson, C. 1999. *The Differentiated Classroom: Responding to the Needs of All Learners*. Alexandria, VA: ASCD.

Tornrose, H. 2004. Personal communication. Yarmouth, ME.

Tyler, R. 1949. *Basic Principles of Curriculum and Instruction.* Chicago: University of Chicago Press.

Vygotsky, L. S. 1962. *Thought and Language.* Cambridge, MA: MIT Press.

Vygotsky, L. S. 1978. *Mind in Society: The Development of Higher Psychological Processes.* Cambridge, MA: Harvard University Press.

Walters, J., S. Seidel, and H. Gardner. 1994. Children as reflective practitioners. In J. N. Mangieri and C. C. Block (Eds.), *Creating Powerful Thinking in Teachers and Students: Diverse Perspectives* (pp. 289–303). Fort Worth, TX: Harcourt Brace College Publishers.

Werner, E. and R. Smith. 1992. *Overcoming the Odds: High Risk Children From Birth to Adulthood.* Ithaca, NY: Cornell University Press.

Wiggins, G. 1993. *Assessing Student Performance: Exploring the Purpose and Limits of Testing.* San Francisco: Jossey-Bass.

Wiggins, G. and J. McTighe. 1998. *Understanding by Design.* Alexandria, VA: ASCD.

Wolf, D. 1987. Opening up assessment. *Educational Leadership* 45, no. 4: 24–29.

Wolf, D. 1989. Portfolio assessment: Sampling student work. *Educational Leadership* 46, no. 7: 35–39.

Wolfe, P. 2001. *Brain Matters: Translating the Research to Classroom Practice.* Alexandria, VA: ASCD.

Young, E. 2000. *Enhancing Student Writing by Teaching Self-Assessment Strategies that Incorporate the Criteria of Good Writers.* Doctoral dissertation. New Brunswick, NJ: Rutgers University Graduate School of Education.

Zessoules, R. and H. Gardner. 1991. Authentic assessment: Beyond the buzzword and into the classroom. In V. Perrone (Ed.), *Expanding Student Assessment* (pp. 47–71). Alexandria, VA: ASCD.

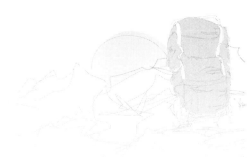

Appendix 1: Research Summaries and Connections

We are often asked who to read and what to read. In appendix 1, we have summarized key bodies of research that we hope will help you deepen your own work as a leader. This is just a starting point. As leaders, we need to continually expand the volume and scope of our reading in order to better support the learning of others and the organizations in which we work.

Research Summaries and Connections

Involving Students in Assessment: Research Summary

Research shows that when students are involved in their own assessment, they learn more. Student involvement in assessment has many different looks and may include students:

- Co-constructing criteria and looking at samples of student work to better understand quality and what is needed for success
- Self-assessing and giving themselves timely feedback
- Engaging in productive learning conversations with peers
- Asking themselves questions that guide their thinking
- Thinking about their learning as they articulate their understanding
- Coming to see mistakes as feedback and a natural part of the learning process
- Making choices about what to focus on as they have an opportunity to identify next steps and set goals
- Selecting evidence of their own learning, considering strengths and areas to improve, and explaining their thinking to others
- Being involved in their own assessment and providing teachers with more information so teachers can better design instruction to meet their needs

In summary, research over many years has consistently shown that when students are involved in their own assessment they learn to self-monitor and self-regulate, which are important elements of success in school and in life.

Research Favorites

To find examples and discussions of involving students in their own assessment, look to the literature that focuses on reflection, metacognition, self-regulation, feedback, assessment *for* learning, and learning. Consider beginning with the following readings:

Andrade, H. 2011. Foreword. In K. Gregory, C. Cameron, and A. Davies, *Self-Assessment and Goal Setting*, 2nd Edition, pp. 7–16. Bloomington, IN: Solution Tree Press.

Black, P. and D. Wiliam. 1998. Assessment and classroom learning. *Assessment in Education* 5, no. 1: 7–75.

Davies, A. 2011. *Making Classroom Assessment Work*, 3rd Edition. Bloomington, IN: Solution Tree Press.

Dweck, C. S. 2000. *Self-Theories: Their Role in Motivation, Personality and Development.* Philadelphia: The Psychology Press.

Stiggins, R. 2004. *Student-Involved Assessment for Learning*, 4th Edition. Upper Saddle River, NJ: Pearson Prentice Hall.

Feedback for Learning: Research Summary

Research is overwhelmingly clear. The more specific, descriptive feedback students receive, the more they learn; the more evaluative feedback students receive, especially if they struggle, the less they will learn (Black and Wiliam 1998; Butler 1987, 1988; Crooks 1988; Hattie and Timperley 2007). Hattie (1992) explains, "The most powerful single moderator that enhances achievement is feedback. . . . It means providing information how and why the child understands and misunderstands, and what direction the student must take to improve" (p. 4).

Shepard (2000) explains that how we think about feedback in education has changed. Students receive different kinds of feedback, and each has a different impact on learning (Butler 1987, 1988). *Descriptive feedback* comes during, as well as after, the learning. It is easily understood and relates directly to the learning. It is specific so performance can improve. It involves choice on the part of the learner as to the type of feedback and how to receive it. It is part of an ongoing conversation about the learning. It is often given in comparison to models, exemplars, samples, or descriptions. *Evaluative feedback* often comes at the end of the learning. It tells the learner how she or he has performed compared to others (norm-referenced assessment) or what was to be learned (criterion-referenced assessment). Evaluative feedback is communicated using letters, numbers, checks, or other symbols; it is encoded. Students usually understand whether or not they need to improve. Unless students can decode the evaluative feedback, they do not have enough information to understand what they need to do differently in order to improve.

Research Favorites

Black, P. and D. Wiliam. 1998. Assessment and classroom learning. *Assessment in Education* 5, no. 1: 7–75.

Butler, R. 1987. Task-involving and ego-involving properties of evaluation: Effects of different feedback conditions on motivational perceptions, interest and performance. *Journal of Educational Psychology* 79, no. 4: 474–482.

Butler, R. 1988. Enhancing and undermining intrinsic motivation: The effects of task-involving and ego-involving evaluation on interest and performance. *British Journal of Educational Psychology,* 58: 1–14.

Hattie, J. 2008. *Visible Learning: A Synthesis of Over 800 Meta-Analyses Relating to Achievement.* New York: Routledge.

Hattie, J. and H. Timperley. 2007. The power of feedback. *Review of Educational Research* 77, no. 1: 81–112.

Shepard, L. 2000. The role of assessment in a learning culture. *Educational Researcher* 29, no. 7: 4–14.

Grades, Percentages, and Other Symbols: Research Summary

Researchers report that grades and other symbols that communicate evaluative feedback have a negative effect on learning for all students. Over the years, research has persistently shown negative effects are most pronounced with low-achieving students (Butler 1987, 1988; Butterworth and Michael 1975; Calkins 1991; Curwin 1978; Harter 1978; Kyle 1992; Natriello 1984).

Research shows that students of high ability and high achievement decode evaluative feedback so it provides information that assists learning (Brookhart 2001). Specific descriptive feedback that focuses on what was done successfully and points the way to improvement has a positive effect on learning.

Students with poor grades are more likely to see themselves as failures. They are less likely to succeed as learners. Further, limiting specific feedback means students have less information to support their future learning. It appears that because grades and other symbols give many students the message that they are not able learners, they become less successful at school (Deci and Ryan 2002; Harlen and Deakin Crick 2003; Kohn 1999).

Therefore, when possible, refrain from giving evaluative feedback such as grades, percentages, and other symbols. When grades, marks, and symbols must be used (e.g., many report cards require them), taking the time to help all students learn to decode evaluative feedback so that it gives them specific information to support their learning (e.g., "do more of this, do less of this") is important. One way to do this is by defining grades and other symbols by providing a detailed description of the quality of the evidence that results in different grades, marks, or symbols.

Research Favorites

Black, P. and D. Wiliam. 1998. Assessment and classroom learning. *Assessment in Education* 5, no. 1: 7–75.

Brookhart, S. 2001. Successful students' formative and summative uses of assessment information. *Assessment in Education* 8, no. 21: 153–169.

Butler, R. 1987. Task-involving and ego-involving properties of evaluation: Effects of different feedback conditions on motivational perceptions, interest and performance. *Journal of Educational Psychology* 79, no. 4: 474–482.

Butler, R. 1988. Enhancing and undermining intrinsic motivation: The effects of task-involving and ego-involving evaluation on interest and performance. *British Journal of Educational Psychology.* 58: 1–14.

Harlen, W. and R. Deakin Crick. 2002. *Testing, Motivation and Learning.* Booklet produced by ARG at University of Cambridge Faculty of Education. http://www.assessment-reform-group.org/TML%20BOOKLET%20complete.pdf

Harlen, W. and R. Deakin Crick. 2003. Testing and motivation for learning. *Assessment in Education* 10, no. 2: 169–208.

Retention in Grade: Research Summary

In spite of research over the years consistently showing the negative effects of retention in grade, the practice continues. Holmes, in 1989, conducted a meta-analysis and found that while retainees did improve during the first year they were retained, three years later there were almost no differences and no academic benefits for retention. Retained children were no better off in relation to their younger at-risk controls who went immediately on to the next grade. Researchers have also found that failure depresses action potential, slows learning, causes a moving away from reality, causes persistent nonadjusting behavior, has a cumulative effect, causes changes in attitude, makes children less able to remember, and has a negative effect on interactions with parents. Some highlights:

- In specific studies on kindergarten and retention (Niklason 1987; Shepard and Smith 1989) and children born in the last quarter of the year (Funk 1969), researchers reported no benefits to children.
- More boys than girls are retained, regardless of intelligence indicators (Cantalini 1987; Ellis 1968; Funk 1969; Peterson, De Gracie, and Ayabe 1987; Shepard and Smith 1989).
- Children retained in one school may not have been retained in another school within the same district (Overman 1986).
- Retention with remediation has been tried and failed (Gredler 1984; Niklason 1987). A study of grade 1, 2, and 3 students found that while retainees did improve during the first year they were retained, three years later there were almost no differences and

no academic benefits for retention (Peterson, De Gracie, and Ayabe 1987).

- Children kept in a transition class did not perform better than a control group over a three-year period (Shepard and Smith 1987).

Research Favorites

Hattie, J. 1992. Measuring the effects of schooling. *Australian Journal of Education* 36, no. 1: 5–13.

Holmes, C. T. 1989. Grade level retention effects: A meta-analysis of research studies. In L. A. Shepard and M. L. Smith (Eds.), *Flunking Grades: The Policies and Effects of Retention*, pp. 16–33. London, UK: Falmer Press.

Shepard, L. A. and M. L. Smith. 1987. What doesn't work: Explaining policies of retention in the early grades. *Phi Delta Kappan* 69 (October): 129–134.

Shepard, L. A. and M. L. Smith. 1989. *Flunking Grades: Research and Policies on Retention.* New York: Falmer Press.

Tracking and Ability Grouping: Research Summary

Tracking refers to the practice of dividing students into groups, based on perceived ability, for some or all of the school day and then providing a set curriculum, provided at the same pace for all students in the classroom.

Research over the years has shown that when students are tracked or placed in inflexible ability groups, they learn less and have more limited opportunities to access future learning (Dornbusch 1994; Oakes 1985; Tieso 2003). The use of whole class ability grouping disproportionately impacts minority students, economically disadvantaged students, and students with lower ability. The practice of whole class ability grouping and tracking can deny children their right to equal educational opportunity. When schools have been de-tracked and or when other structures are employed (see facing page), incidences of violence have reduced dramatically and schools have seen increases in test scores and achievement levels.

Assessment for *Learning:* When students are involved in the assessment process—setting criteria, self-assessing, peer feedback, collecting evidence, showing proof of learning—they learn more (Black and Wiliam 1998).

Curriculum Modification: More students are supported to learn by removing repetitive, unnecessary, and unchallenging content; enhancing existing curricular materials with higher-level questioning and critical thinking; and purposefully assisting students to see the relevance and to transfer skills and insights into different contexts (Brooks and Brooks 1993; Erickson 1998; Wiggins and McTighe 1998).

Scaffolding Instruction: Providing opportunities for both guided and independent practice supports student learning (Langer and Applebee 1986; Palincsar and Brown 1986).

Flexible Grouping: Used sparingly, flexible grouping can be effective when student progress is monitored closely, and groups are continually remixed (Marzano, Pickering, and Pollock 2001).

Differentiated Instruction: The practice of differentiated instruction allows all students equal access to the curriculum, while maintaining high expectations for students (Kulik and Kulik 1992; Tomlinson 1999).

Small-Group Instruction: Remediation, direct instruction, monitoring student mastery of educational concepts, and accommodating individual learning needs is more possible when teachers utilize small-group instruction (Marzano 2000; Slavin 1996; Springer, Stanne, and Donovan 1999).

Cooperative Learning Strategies: When students work collaboratively to successfully achieve a desired educational outcome, they develop a greater understanding and respect for individual differences, and they learn more (Aronson 1972; Slavin 1996).

Research Favorites

Dornbusch, S. 1994. School tracking harms millions, sociologist finds. *Stanford University News Service.* March 2, 1994. http://www.stanford.edu/dept/news/pr/94/940302Arc4396.html

Oakes, J. 1985. *Keeping Track: How Schools Structure Inequality*. New Haven, CT: Yale University Press.

Shepard, L. 2000. The role of assessment in a learning culture. *Educational Researcher* 29, no. 7: 4–14.

Slavin, R. E. 1987. Ability grouping and student achievement in elementary schools: A best-evidence synthesis. *Review of Educational Research*, 57, no. 3: 293–336.

Slavin, R. E. 1990. Achievement effects of ability grouping in secondary schools: A best-evidence synthesis. *Review of Educational Research*, 60, no. 3: 471–499.

One-to-One Access to Technology: Research Summary

Research on technology implementation is mixed as to its impact on student achievement scores, with some studies showing a positive impact, and others showing little, if any, difference. When studies with one-to-one computing are examined, the results change dramatically, showing improved writing scores (Jeroski 2003; Lowther, Ross and Morrison 2001; Rockman 2003; Rockman et al. 2000; Russell et al. 2002) and improved test scores (Hill et al. 2002; Light et al. 2002; Lowther, Ross and Morrison 2001). In spite of these positive results, there is little information concerning how well the tests reflect the student learning in a one-to-one computing classroom.

Research connected with learning and technology changes rapidly as new technologies and new practices are investigated. If we consider that learning is constructed over time as a result of experience, interaction with others, and reflection, then the research questions pursued focus on experience, interactions, and reflection. One-to-one classrooms can change the relationships between students and students, students and adults, and students and outside resources (digital and human). They also provide a richer "zone of proximal development"—a phrase used by Vygotsky (1978) to capture learning occurring in a social setting. Research findings indicate that more students can experience an environment supportive of their learning in a one-to-one situation because they have more influence over factors that contribute to learning.

As we consider how technology changes *how* students go about their learning, *what* students learn, and the *student's personal context* for learning, new questions emerge. Students seek more feedback, they work toward success using feedback from self and others to guide their learning, and they express an *intention* to learn, using feedback to achieve success. The result is that the kind, quantity, and quality of the evidence of student learning changes. The role students have in showing proof of their learning is changing. The role teachers have in showing proof of student learning is changing. The significance of these changes needs to continue to be explored.

Since learning is a process of construction that requires active engagement on the part of the learner, this context of one-to-one computing is likely to result in more student learning (Papert 1999) because students are engaged, making mistakes, producing work, making choices, tailoring learning to meet their learning needs, pacing their own learning, and having access to current, relevant information. And, if one considers Sugata Mitra's work, the interaction between learners is of critical importance. Further, consider the role of practice. Technology access allows students to differentiate for themselves the amount and kind of practice. Ericsson et al. (1993) write about the role of deliberate practice in the acquisition of expertise.

In summary, the lessons we are learning regarding technology, learning, and instruction continue. We all need to be researchers when it comes to understanding more fully what supports learning and learners.

Research Favorites

Davies, A. 2004. *Finding Proof of Learning in a One-to-One Computing Classroom*. Courtenay, BC: Connections Publishing.

Ericsson, K. A., R. T. Krampe, and C. Tesch-Rome. 1993. The role of deliberate practice in the acquisition of expert performance. *Psychological Review* 100, no. 3: 363–406.

Mitra, S. Consider viewing: http://www.ted.com/speakers/sugata_ mitra.html

Silvernail, D. L. 2005. *Does Maine's Middle School Laptop Program Improve Learning? A Review of Evidence to Date.* University of Southern Maine, Center for Education Policy, Applied Research, and Evaluation. Retrieved from http://usm.maine.edu/sites/default/files/Center%20for%20Education%20Policy,%20Applied%20Research,%20and%20Evaluation/MLTI705.pdf.

Classroom Tests: Research Summary

More testing may mean less learning. Measurement alone is not enough, there needs to be intervention. Over the years, researchers have said that testing does not improve student learning (Black and Wiliam 1998; Stiggins 2004; Rothman 1995), and further, that testing may result in decreased learning (Harlen and Deakin Crick 2003; Lieberman and Langer 1995).

There are many reasons why educators need to be careful as they consider test results. For example, errors in student responses on a test may be due largely to misunderstandings by participants rather than their lack of knowledge. Both taking tests and scoring tests are interpretive processes. Thus, a student's poor performance may be due to the structure of the test rather than lack of ability.

Further, tests that require simple responses (e.g., multiple choice, true/false, or short answer) are not objective measures of student learning. These kinds of assessments can indicate certain information when used properly, but cannot be used to measure *all* important knowledge, abilities, and skills (Stiggins 2004). For example, when teachers choose to emphasize one part of the curriculum over another, select test items, and determine the weightings for various questions, they build subjectivity into the tests they create.

Quality assessment cannot be limited to recall (e.g., paper-and-pencil tests) because learning is more than recitation; assessment must also include observation of demonstrations and talking with learners about their understandings.

Research Favorites

Black, P. and D. Wiliam. 1998. Assessment and classroom learning. *Assessment in Education* 5, no. 1: 7–75.

Lieberman, M. and E. J. Langer. 1995. Mindfulness in the process of learning. In E. J. Langer (Ed.), *The Power of Mindful Learning*. Reading, MA: Addison-Wesley.

Stiggins, R. 2004. *Student-Centered Classroom Assessment*, 4th Edition. Upper Saddle River, NJ: Pearson Prentice Hall.

Large-Scale Assessments: Research Summary

High-quality large-scale assessments are expensive. Many jurisdictions start with high-quality assessments, but reduce the number of performance test items in order to reduce expenses. As a result, the tests no longer reflect the breadth of the program of studies in schools. Over time it has been reported that the tendency is to only include those items that are easy to assess in a multiple-test format. Over time, researchers have reported that large-scale assessments designed to assess how well students are learning the curriculum fall far short of their target because much of the curriculum cannot be adequately tested by "paper-and-pencil" tests (ARG 2006; Shepard 1989; Stiggins 2004; Wiggins 1993).

Reliability and validity of large-scale assessments are determined differently than for classroom assessment. Large-scale assessments effectively report on what groups of students are learning. However, because not enough information is collected in relation to all the learning standards or outcomes, the results are not valid when considering individuals in the test population (ARG 2006; Stiggins 2004). This means large-scale test results must be carefully interpreted and used in concert with classroom generated data to give a more complete picture of a student's learning.

Large-scale standardized tests can be a poor measure of student learning because the content is negotiated to reflect needs of diverse groups, such as several states or provinces; content is narrowed to reduce the number of questions and the time needed to write the test; multiple-choice formats (which can only assess some kinds of learning) are used; and teachers may limit their teaching to what is likely to be on the test (ARG 2006; Shepard 1989).

Research Favorites

ARG. (Harlen, W.). 2006. *The Role of Teachers in the Assessment of Learning*. Pamphlet produced by Assessment Systems for the Future project (ASF) Assessment Reform Group, UK. http://www.assessment-reform-group.org/ASF%20 booklet%20English.pdf

Shepard, L. 2000. The role of assessment in a learning culture. *Educational Researcher* 29, no. 7: 4–14.

Stiggins, R. 2004. *Student-Centered Classroom Assessment*, 4th Edition. Upper Saddle River, NJ: Pearson Prentice Hall.

Intelligence and Intelligence Tests: Research Summary

Intelligence as measured by tests is no longer viewed as innate and unchangeable. Tests that claim to measure and quantify intelligence often do not. Such tests tend to focus on measuring certain kinds of attributes that are simply good predictors of success in schools, i.e., memorization and academic skills, and confidence in test taking. Scores on multiple-choice intelligence tests are not good predictors of success—they are good predictors of scores on subsequent similar tests (Goleman 1996; Gould 1981; Jensen 1998; Sternberg 1986).

As a result, intelligence as measured by tests can be modified—increased or decreased. The brain can change itself and make itself smarter—more able to learn, to know, to do, and to articulate (Doidge 2007). Schooling is one factor that can change intelligence test results. Opportunities for social contact; high-challenge, low-stress experiences; and experiences in novel situations can increase scores on intelligence tests. Intelligence during the school years appears to be dynamic, and it is affected by environmental factors, particularly access to high-quality schooling (Berliner & Biddle 1998; Goleman 1996).

Schooling affects performance on intelligence tests. High-quality instructional environments for toddlers, primary-school children, teenagers, and college students all tend to raise scores on intelligence tests. One researcher argues that a child could lose as many as six IQ points for each year of high-quality education missed (Ceci 1990; Gould 1981; Sternberg 1996). Some researchers argue that when we track students based on IQ, we condemn them to "stunted mental growth" (Berliner and Biddle 1998).

Research Favorites

ARG. (Harlen, W.). 2006. *The Role of Teachers in the Assessment of Learning*. Pamphlet produced by Assessment Systems for the Future project (ASF) Assessment Reform Group, UK. http://www.assessment-reform-group.org/ASF%20 booklet%20English.pdf

Berliner, D. and B. Biddle. 1998. *The Manufactured Crisis: Myths, Frauds and the Attack on America's Public Schools.* New York: Longman.

Gould, S. J. 1981. *The Mismeasure of Man.* New York: Norton.

Motivation and Rewards: Research Summary

Mastery-learning-oriented students challenge themselves to learn. When teachers focus on the learning and actual performance, they support students to continue to be intrinsically motivated and encourage them to take risks. Specific, descriptive feedback fosters interest and creativity and can lead to increased intrinsic motivation. The result is more learning (Covington 1998; Deci and Ryan 2002; Dweck 2000).

Rewards undermine interest and motivation and can lead to students being performance-goal-oriented (also referred to as extrinsically motivated). Extrinsically motivated students tend to select tasks that are low in difficulty. Rewarded behaviors are often short-lived. At risk are both students who experience repeated failure, rejection, and alienation and those who believe they are worthy only as a result of external proof of superiority (Deci and Ryan 1985; Harlen and Deakin Crick 2003).

Rewards, such as grades, points, marks, praise, or any kind of evaluative feedback, can lead to less-than-ideal learning environments.

Assessment research shows they can interrupt the learning of students who struggle (Butler 1987, 1988). Further, rewards can divert attention from the actual performance and learning. They can interfere with relationships in the learning environment and result in students being less motivated and less willing to take the risks needed to learn (Deci and Ryan, 1985).

Research Favorites

Deci, E. and R. M. Ryan. 2002. *Handbook of Self-Determination Research.* Rochester, NY: University of Rochester Press.

Dweck, C. S. 2000. *Self-Theories: Their Role in Motivation, Personality and Development.* Philadelphia: Psychology Press.

Harlen, W. and R. Deakin Crick. 2003. Testing and motivation for learning. *Assessment in Education* 10, no. 2: 169–208.

Appendix 2:
Reproducibles

The following reproducibles are provided for leaders to adapt to their own use, ensuring that the credits and copyright information appear on every page that is copied.

To enlarge to 8½ x 11 inches, please set photocopier at 115%.

Research Matters

Why involve students? Why consider revisiting classroom assessment and the role of summative assessment? Recent research in this area is clearly pointing towards needed changes. What is the key classroom assessment research that every school leader needs to know about? There are seven important research studies focused on assessment that have often been missed by those planning to measure student achievement and set policies to encourage best teaching and assessment practices.

1. Butler (1987, 1988) conducted experimental design studies and found that student work receiving grades and marks (with or without feedback) was clearly associated with decreasing student achievement, while specific feedback without grades and marks was clearly associated with increasing achievement.

2. Black and Wiliam (1998) summarized classroom assessment research conducted internationally over a ten-year period. Their findings explain the power of classroom assessment and its role in improving learning. They detailed the significant learning achievements students experience—especially struggling students—when assessment *for* learning techniques are employed. Key strategies include setting clear success criteria, increasing specific, descriptive feedback, and decreasing summarized, evaluative feedback such as grades and marks.

3. Harlen and Deakin Crick (2003), studying the role of tests and motivation to learn, found that students who do less well on tests and evaluations of any kind tend to be less motivated and, as a result, do even less well on subsequent tests and evaluations. Based on their research, they strongly recommend that students be engaged in assessment *for* learning activities—such as setting criteria, giving and receiving feedback, and collecting evidence of learning—in order to increase achievement levels, as well as motivation to learn.

4. Meisels et al.'s (2003) study examined the impact of curriculum-embedded performance assessment on students' subsequent performance on the Iowa Tests of Basic Skills (ITBS). The researchers note that obtaining continuous information about students during the learning and engaging students as active participants in the classroom assessment process enhances teaching and improves learning.

5. Rodriguez (2004) "evaluated the relationship between assessment practices and achievement and the mediated roles of students' self-efficacy and effort" (p. 1). Rodriguez found that teachers' classroom assessment practices have a significant relationship to classroom performance. Classroom assessment practices include writing assignments, data collection activities, long- and short-term individual projects, oral reports, worksheets, homework, journal writing, quizzes, tests, observations, student responses in class, and externally created exams that were used to give feedback, group students, diagnose learning problems, and plan future lessons.

6. The Assessment Reform Group in the UK commissioned a series of studies examining summative assessment. Working Papers 1, 2, and 3 are available (ARG-ASF Project, 2005: http://k1.ioe.ac.uk/tlrp/arg/ASF.html). They found when teachers work with each other and review evidence of student learning to determine whether or not students are meeting the standards with sufficient quality, teachers become more confident and better able to make independent judgments. Further, the reliability of teachers' assessment increases when teachers participate in developing criteria, have some ownership of them, and understand the language used. Teachers who learn to assess student work as part of external summative assessment processes using clearly specified criteria improve the quality of their classroom assessment.

7. "Formative Assessment—Improving Student Learning in Secondary Classrooms" (Centre for Educational Research and Innovation 2005), a report based on research findings and classroom-level observations in 8 countries (Australia [Queensland], Denmark, England, Finland, Italy, New Zealand, Scotland, and some provinces in Canada) concluded that classroom assessment that supports student learning:

   • Establishes a classroom culture that encourages interaction and the use of assessment tools
   • Establishes learning goals, and tracks individual student progress toward those goals
   • Uses varied instruction methods to meet diverse student needs
   • Uses varied approaches to assessing student understanding
   • Provides feedback on student performance and adaptation of instruction to meet identified needs
   • Involves students actively in the learning and assessment process

The research is compelling. School leaders intending to make a difference for students need to focus on classroom assessment.

Adapted from A. Davies, "Leading Towards Learning and Achievement" in J. Burger, C. Webber, and P. Klinck (Eds.). 2007. *Intelligent Leadership: Constructs for Thinking Education Leaders.* Secaucus, NJ: Springer Publishers.

Reference page 12 in text.

Protocol: Examining Student Work in Relation to
Descriptions of Quality

Facilitator: Ensures group sets ground rules and that time limits are strictly observed. Facilitator observes but does not participate.

Prior Preparation: Presenting teacher (PT) has comprehensive collection of student evidence for one term for one child and a description of success for report card symbol that includes qualitative data as well as quantitative data. Participants (Part) have professional expertise—an understanding of the standards or learning outcomes as well as experience teaching children in this age range.

(PT) 10 minutes: Presenting teacher shows comprehensive collection of student evidence for one term, talks about standards, shares the description, but does not talk about the child. When finished, the presenting teacher moves his/her chair back from the group and begins to take notes.

(Part) 15 minutes: Participants describe what they see in the work. What do they notice? What questions do they have? (PT does not respond at this time.)

(Part) 15 minutes: Participants identify the standards they see being evidenced by the collection of work, score the work using the description of a letter grade provided by the presenting teacher, and provide reasons for the score. (PT does not respond at this time.)

(PT) 10 minutes: Presenting teacher rejoins the group. Group members listen to presenting teacher describe the collection of student work more fully, respond to questions, and add information.

(Part) 10 minutes: Participants discuss the implications for assessment, evaluation, and instruction.

(All) 7 minutes: Everyone mentally steps back, reflects, records their thoughts regarding this protocol (in writing, silently), and then shares their thoughts verbally.

PT: Presenting Teacher
Part: Participants

Adapted from with permission from *Protocols for Professional Learning Conversations* by Catherine Glaude (2011).

Reference page 44 in text.

Learning Conversations: Sticky Issues Classroom Assessment Conversation

This conversation is to help participants deepen their understanding and their thinking about classroom assessment issues that currently seem to be sticky issues.

Guidelines:
- Facilitator keeps time and calls time.
- Facilitator reviews or affirms ground rules.
- Facilitator reminds participants of ground rules if needed.
- Remember, this conversation is not about advice; it is about expanding our thinking.
- Unless presenting, do not talk about your school or your situation.

Groups of 4 Plus Facilitator:
Record on an index card a sticky issue you have at this time with regard to classroom assessment. Write a few lines about your dilemma. Then, frame the sticky issue into a question. Review all the sticky issues. Select one person and his/her sticky issue to begin.

1. A presents a sticky issue concerning classroom assessment. (5 minutes) Record the sticky issue on the board/chart so everyone can refer to it. Talk about the dilemma you face. B, C, & D are silent.
2. B, C, & D ask clarifying questions. A answers briefly. (3 minutes)
3. B, C, & D discuss what they have heard about the dilemma. A is silent. A listens and takes notes about what is being said that is helping stretch his/her thinking about the dilemma. Their dialogue focuses on the following:
   - What seems to be the primary issue?
   - What questions does the sticky issue raise for you?
   - What didn't you hear that you wonder about? (8 minutes)
4. A speaks to what was said that helped to stretch her/his thinking. Others are silent as she/he speaks.
5. A, B, C, & D closure. (4 minutes) Start with A sharing how the process helped her with the issue. Then B, C, and D comment.
6. Facilitator calls time and closes.

Break:
After a short stretch, invite another participant to present his/her sticky issue.

Process adapted from Sticky Issue protocol developed by Southern Maine Partnership and found in Critical Friends Toolbox. www.essentialschools.org

Reference page 71 in text.

Closing the Achievement Gap

Self-Assessment Checklist for Learner Involvement

	Met	On the Way	Beginning	Evidence
1. Learners are able to articulate the learning destination and understand what success looks like.				
2. Learners have access to samples that show quality work.				
3. Learners are able to describe what evidence of learning might look like.				
4. Learners set criteria *with* teachers to define quality.				
5. Learners have time to learn.				
6. Learners receive and give themselves specific, descriptive feedback as they learn.				
7. Learners debrief their learning with their peers and others and get feedback for learning.				
8. Learners use feedback and self-assess to set goals for future learning.				
9. Learners revisit and reset the criteria as they learn more.				
10. Learners collect evidence of their own learning.				
11. Learners present evidence of learning to others and receive feedback. They have opportunities to improve the quality of their evidence of learning. Evaluation is based on evidence collected from multiple sources over time.				
12. Learners are authentically engaged in the learning/assessment process. They are working harder and learning more.				
13. Reports are based on triangulated data (multiple sources).				

Reference page 73 in text.

Sample Selection Protocol

Purpose of the Protocol: To collect a range of samples that represents work from a grade level.

Prior to the Conversation: The facilitator identifies a focus question (i.e., Would you agree that this work represents the range of work—developing, on the way, exceeding—for this grade level?)

(2 minutes)
Getting Started: Select a facilitator and a timekeeper. Review the purpose of the protocol and ground rules for this process. Be sure everyone has brought samples created by students in response to the same task. Note: student and teacher names should be removed.

(5 minutes)
Context: The facilitator offers any background information and the purpose for the assessment. The focus question is written on chart paper or board for all to see.

(5 minutes)
Review: The group members review the student work in regard to the focus question. (If student work is lengthy, the work and the focus question may be given ahead of time.)

(12 minutes)
Group Discussion: Using the focus question as their guide, group members generate their insights and observations by what they see in the work. The facilitator moderates the discussion.

(5 minutes)
The group selects and organizes two or three samples as exemplars of each level (e.g., developing, on the way, exceeding) to show the range of work found at the grade level in response to the task.

(5 minutes)
Reflection on the Conversation: The group discusses how they experienced this protocol conversation and what they learned.

Adapted with permission from *Protocols for Professional Learning Conversations* by Catherine Glaude (2011).

Reference page 97 in text.

Reviewing Reporting Process

Questions to Consider	Notes
Are you working within the legal requirements for evaluation and reporting to community and/or state/provincial education authorities?	
Have you developed an assessment plan for each school or district goal/priority?	
Do you have a collaboratively developed description of what success looks like?	
How is your staff involved in the assessment process?	
Are you collecting evidence over time so that growth can be noted along the way and, if necessary, adjustments can be made?	
How is your staff involved in collecting and organizing the evidence? Have responsibilities been assigned to various members of your team?	
What evidence does your team examine, and how do you evaluate evidence of results against your stated goals, in preparation for reporting?	
Do your immediate staff and others in your school/system understand what is being evaluated?	
Are reports written in language that educational partners can understand?	
How do you share the reports and results both within and outside the school/district?	
Do you include information regarding gaps or problems that have been identified through the collection of evidence?	

Reference page 121 in text.

Anne Davies, Ph.D., is a researcher, writer, and educational consultant. She has also been a teacher, school administrator, and system leader. Anne has taught at universities both in Canada and the United States, including University of Victoria and University of Southern Maine. Anne is the author of more than 30 books and multimedia resources, as well as numerous chapters and articles. Since 2001, Anne has been a member of the team representing Canada at the International Conference on Assessment *for* Learning. It has been held in United Kingdom (2001), United States (2004), New Zealand (2009), and Norway (2011). A recipient of the Hilroy Fellowship for Innovative Teaching, Anne continues to support others to learn more about assessment in the service of learning and learners.

Sandra Herbst is a noted system leader, author, speaker, and consultant with over twenty years of experience. She has worked in both elementary and secondary schools and is a former classroom and specialty teacher, school administrator, program consultant, and assistant superintendent and is a past president of the Manitoba Association of School Superintendents. Sandra has facilitated professional learning in schools, districts, and organizations across North America in the areas of leadership, instruction, assessment, and evaluation. Her school and district experiences deeply connect learners to practical and possible strategies and approaches. She is the co-author of two books on the topic of assessment.

Beth Parrott Reynolds, Ph.D., is the president and performance consultant for Leadership for Learning, Inc. and a practicing school improvement specialist. She is a former English teacher, high school principal, and assistant superintendent with more than 30 years of experience in leading schools and districts to develop the internal capacity needed to drive change for student and organizational success. In addition to keynotes, Beth is often asked to lead deep work with schools and districts in areas including standards, assessment, instruction, and grading. She is the co-author of two books on the topic of assessment.